MW01709944

Albert Einstein
Father of Modern Physics

Albert Einstein
Father of Modern Physics

By
P. K. Das
M. K. Singh

MP
MAHAVEER PUBLISHERS

Published by
MAHAVEER PUBLISHERS
4764/2A, 23-Ansari Road, Daryaganj
New Delhi – 110002
Ph. : 011 – 66629669–79–89
e-mail : mahaveerpublishers@gmail.com

First Edition : October 2012

Albert Einstein
ISBN : 9789350880036

Distributed in India by
VAIBHAV BOOK SERVICE
e-mail : vaibhavbookservice@gmail.com

Distributed in Nepal by
BAJRANGBALI BOOK ENTERPRISES PVT. LTD.
Jyatha Mushyabahal, Ward No. 27, Kathmandu, Nepal
e-mail : bajrangbalibooks@gmail.com

Printed in India

Introduction

Albert Einstein was a theoretical physicist. His many contributions to physics include the special and general theories of relativity, the founding of relativistic cosmology, the first post-Newtonian expansion, explaining the perihelion advance of Mercury, prediction of the deflection of light by gravity and gravitational lensing, the first fluctuation dissipation theorem which explained the Brownian movement of molecules, the photon theory and wave-particle duality, the quantum theory of atomic motion in solids, the zero-point energy concept, the semiclassical version of the Schrödinger equation, and the quantum theory of a monatomic gas which predicted Bose-Einstein condensation.

Einstein is best known for his theories of special relativity and general relativity. He received the 1921 Nobel Prize in Physics "for his services to Theoretical Physics, and especially for his discovery of the law of the photoelectric effect."

Einstein published more than 300 scientific and over 150 non-scientific works. He is often regarded as the father of modern physics.

Albert Einstein, 1921

Contents

Early Life and Education

Albert Einstein was born in Ulm, in the Kingdom of Württemberg in the German Empire on 14 March 1879. His father was Hermann Einstein, a salesman and an engineer. His mother was Pauline Einstein (née Koch). In 1880, the family moved to Munich, where his father and his uncle founded *Elektrotechnische Fabrik J. Einstein & Cie*, a company that manufactured electrical equipment based on direct current.

Albert Einstein in 1893 (age 14). From Euclid, Einstein began to understand deductive reasoning, and by the age of twelve, he had learned Euclidean geometry. Soon after he began to investigate infinitesimal calculus. At age 16, he performed the first of his famous *thought experiments* in which he visualized travelling alongside a beam of light.

The Einsteins were non-observant Jews. Their son attended a Catholic elementary school from the age of five until ten. Although Einstein had early speech difficulties, he was a top student in elementary school. As he grew, Einstein built models and mechanical devices for fun and began to show a talent for mathematics. In 1889 Max Talmud (later changed to Max Talmey) introduced the ten-year old Einstein to key texts in science, mathematics and philosophy, including Kant's *Critique of Pure Reason* and Euclid's *Elements* (which Einstein called the "holy little geometry book"). Talmud was a poor Jewish medical student from Poland. The Jewish community arranged for Talmud to take meals with the Einsteins each week on Thursdays for six years. During this time Talmud wholeheartedly guided Einstein through many secular educational interests.

In 1894, his father's company failed: Direct current (DC) lost the War of Currents to alternating current (AC). In search of business, the Einstein family moved to Italy, first to Milan and then, a few months later, to Pavia. When the family moved to Pavia, Einstein stayed in Munich to finish his studies at the Luitpold Gymnasium. His father intended for him to pursue electrical engineering, but Einstein clashed with authorities and resented the school's regimen and teaching method. He later wrote that the spirit of learning and creative thought were lost in strict rote learning. In the spring of 1895, he withdrew to join his family in Pavia, convincing the school to let him go by using a doctor's note. During this time, Einstein wrote his first scientific work, "The Investigation of the State of Aether in Magnetic Fields".

Einstein applied directly to the Eidgenössische Polytechnische Schule (later Eidgenössische Technische Hochschule (ETH)) in Zürich, Switzerland. Lacking the requisite Matura certificate, he took an entrance examination, which he failed, although he got exceptional marks in mathematics and physics. The Einsteins sent Albert to Aarau, in northern Switzerland to finish secondary school. While lodging with the family of Professor Jost Winteler, he fell in love with the family's daughter, Marie. (His sister Maja later married the Winteler son, Paul.) In Aarau, Einstein studied Maxwell's electromagnetic theory. At age 17, he graduated, and, with his father's approval, renounced his citizenship in the German Kingdom of Württemberg to avoid military service, and enrolled in 1896 in the mathematics and physics program at the Polytechnic in Zurich. Marie Winteler moved to Olsberg, Switzerland for a teaching post.

In the same year, Einstein's future wife, Mileva Maric, also entered the Polytechnic to study mathematics and physics, the only woman in the academic cohort. Over the next few years, Einstein and Maric's friendship developed into romance. Einstein graduated in 1900 from the Polytechnic with a diploma in mathematics and physics; Although historians have debated whether Maric influenced Einstein's work, the majority of academic historians of science agree that she did not.

Marriages and Children

Einstein and Maric married in January 1903, and in May 1904 the couple's first son, Hans Albert Einstein, was born in Bern, Switzerland. Their second son, Eduard, was born in Zurich in July 1910. In 1914, Einstein moved to Berlin, while his wife remained in Zurich with their sons. Maric and Einstein divorced on 14 February 1919, having lived apart for five years. Einstein married Elsa Löwenthal (née Einstein) on 2 June 1919, after having had a relationship with her since 1912. She was his first cousin maternally and his second cousin paternally. In 1933, they immigrated permanently to the United States. In 1935, Elsa Einstein was diagnosed with heart and kidney problems and died in December 1936.

In early 1902, Einstein and Mileva Maric had a daughter they called Lieserl in their correspondence, who was born in Novi Sad where the parents of Mileva lived. Her full name is not known, and her fate is uncertain after 1903.

Lieserl was the first child of Mileva Maric and Albert Einstein. According to the correspondence between her parents, "Lieserl" was born in January, 1902, a year before her parents married, in Novi Sad, Vojvodina, present day Republic of Serbia, and was cared for by her mother for a short time while Einstein worked in Switzerland before Maric joined him there without the child.

"Lieserl's" existence was unknown to biographers until 1986, when a batch of letters between Albert and Mileva was discovered by Hans Albert Einstein's daughter Evelyn.

Maric had hoped for a girl, while Einstein would have preferred a boy. In their letters, they called the unborn child "Lieserl", when referring to a girl, or "Hanserl", if a boy. Both "Lieserl" and "Hanserl" are diminutives of the very common German names Liese (Elisabeth) and Hans (Johannes).

The first reference to Maric's pregnancy is found in a letter Einstein wrote to her from Winterthur, probably on May 28, 1901 (letter 36), asking twice about "the boy" and "our little son", whereas Maric's first reference is found in her letter of November 13, 1901 (letter 43) from Stein am Rhein, in which she refers to the unborn child as "Lieserl". Einstein goes along with Maric's wish for a daughter, and refers to the unborn child as "Lieserl" as well, but with a sense of humour as in letter 45 of December 12, 1901 "... and be happy about our Lieserl, whom I secretly (so Dollie doesn't notice) prefer to imagine a Hanserl."

The child must have been born shortly before February 4, 1902, when Einstein wrote: "... now you see that it really is a Lieserl, just as you'd wished. Is she healthy and does she cry properly?

I love her so much and don't even know her yet!"

The last time "Lieserl" is mentioned in their extant correspondence in Einstein's letter of September 19, 1903 (letter 54), in which he shows concern for her suffering from scarlet fever. His asking "as what is the child registered? [Adding] we must take precautions that problems don't arise for her later" may indicate the intention to give the child up for adoption.

As neither the full name, nor the fate of the child are known so far several theories about her life and death have been put forward:

- Michele Zackheim, in her book on "Lieserl", Einstein's Daughter, states that "Lieserl" was mentally challenged at birth, and that she lived with her mother's family and probably died of scarlet fever in September 1903.
- Another possibility, favoured by Robert Schulmann of the Einstein Papers Project, is that "Lieserl" was adopted by Maric's close friend, Helene Savic, and was raised by her and lived under the name "Zorka Savic" until the 1990s. Savic did in fact raise a child by the name of Zorka, who was blind from childhood and died in the 1990s. Her grandson Milan Popovic rejects the possibility that it was "Lieserl", and also favours the theory, that the child died in September 1903.

Scientific Career

Throughout his life, Einstein published hundreds of books and articles. Most were about physics, but a few expressed leftist political opinions about pacifism, socialism, and zionism. In addition to the work he did by himself, he also collaborated with other scientists on additional projects including the Bose-Einstein statistics, the Einstein refrigerator and others.

Physics in 1900

Einstein's early papers all come from attempts to demonstrate that atoms exist and have a finite nonzero size. At the time of his first paper in 1902, it was not yet completely accepted by physicists that atoms were real, even though chemists had good evidence ever since Antoine Lavoisier's work a century earlier. The reason physicists were skeptical was because no 19th century theory could fully explain the properties of matter from the properties of atoms.

Ludwig Boltzmann was a leading 19th century atomist physicist, who had struggled for years to gain acceptance for atoms. Boltzmann had given an interpretation of the laws of thermodynamics, suggesting that the law of entropy increase is statistical. In Boltzmann's way of thinking, the entropy is the logarithm of the number of ways a system could be configured inside. The reason the entropy goes up is only because it is more likely for a system to go from a special state with only a few possible internal configurations to a more generic state with many. While Boltzmann's statistical interpretation of entropy is universally accepted today, and Einstein believed it, at the turn of the 20th century it was a minority position.

The statistical idea was most successful in explaining the properties of gases. James Clerk Maxwell, another leading atomist, had found the distribution of velocities of atoms in a gas, and derived the surprising result that the viscosity of a gas should be independent of density. Intuitively, the friction in a gas would seem to go to zero as the density goes to zero, but this is not so, because the mean free path of atoms becomes large at low densities. A subsequent experiment by Maxwell and his wife confirmed this surprising prediction. Other experiments on gases and vacuum, using a rotating slitted drum, showed that atoms in a gas had velocities distributed according to Maxwell's distribution law.

In addition to these successes, there were also inconsistencies. Maxwell noted that at cold temperatures, atomic theory predicted specific heats that are too large. In classical statistical mechanics, every spring-like motion has thermal energy $k_B T$ on average at temperature T, so that the specific heat of every spring is Boltzmann's constant k_B. A monatomic solid with N atoms can be thought of as N little balls representing N atoms attached to each other in a box grid with $3N$ springs, so the specific heat of every solid is $3Nk_B$, a result which became known as the Dulong-Petit law. This law is true at room temperature, but not for colder temperatures. At temperatures near zero, the specific heat goes to zero.

Similarly, a gas made up of a molecule with two atoms can be thought of as two balls on a spring. This spring has energy $k_B T$ at high temperatures, and should contribute an extra k_B to the specific heat. It does at temperatures of about 1000 degrees, but at lower temperature, this contribution disappears. At zero temperature, all other contributions to the specific heat from rotations and vibrations also disappear. This behaviour was inconsistent with classical physics.

The most glaring inconsistency was in the theory of light waves. Continuous waves in a box can be thought of as infinitely many spring-like motions, one for each possible standing wave. Each standing wave has a specific heat of k_B, so the total specific heat of a continuous wave like light should be infinite in classical mechanics. This is obviously wrong, because it would mean that all energy in the universe would be instantly sucked up into light waves, and everything would slow down and stop.

These inconsistencies led some people to say that atoms were not physical, but mathematical. Notable among the skeptics was Ernst Mach, whose positivist philosophy led him to demand that if atoms are real, it should be possible to see them directly. Mach believed that atoms were a useful fiction, that in reality they could be assumed to be infinitesimally small, that Avogadro's number was infinite, or so large that it might as well be infinite, and k_B was infinitesimally small. Certain experiments could then be explained by atomic theory, but other experiments could not, and this is the way it will always be.

Einstein opposed this position. Throughout his career, he was a realist. He believed that a single consistent theory should explain all observation, and that this theory would be a description what was really going on, underneath it all. So he set out to show that the atomic point of view was correct. This led him first to thermodynamics, then to statistical physics, and to the theory of specific heats of solids.

In 1905, while he was working in the patent office, the leading German language physics journal *Annalen der Physik* published four of Einstein's papers. The four papers eventually were recognized as revolutionary, and 1905 became known as Einstein's "Miracle Year", and the papers, as the *Annus Mirabilis Papers*,

Annus Mirabilis papers

The Annus Mirabilis papers (from Latin *annus mirabilis*, "extraordinary year") are the papers of Albert Einstein published in the *Annalen der Physik* scientific journal in 1905.

These four articles contributed substantially to the foundation of modern physics and changed views on space, time, and matter. The *Annus Mirabilis* is often called the "Miracle Year" in English or *Wunderjahr* in German.

Background

At the time the papers were written, Einstein did not have easy access to a complete set of scientific reference materials, although he did regularly read and contribute reviews to *Annalen der Physik*. Additionally, scientific colleagues available to discuss his theories were few. He worked as an examiner at the Patent Office in Bern, Switzerland, and he later said of a co-worker there, Michele Besso, that he "could not have found a better sounding board for his ideas in all of Europe". In addition to co-workers and the other members of the self-styled "Olympian Academy" (Solovine and Habicht), his wife, Mileva Maric, may have had some influence on Einstein's work but how much is unclear. Through these papers, Einstein tackles some of the era's most important physics questions and problems. In 1900, a lecture titled "Nineteenth-Century Clouds over the Dynamical Theory of Heat and Light", by Lord Kelvin, suggested that physics had no satisfactory explanations for the results of the Michelson-Morley experiment and for black body radiation. As introduced, special relativity provided an account for the results of the Michelson-Morley experiments. Einstein's theories for the photoelectric effect extended the quantum theory which Max Planck had developed in his successful explanation of black body radiation.

Despite the greater fame achieved by his other works, such as that on special relativity, it was his work on the photoelectric effect which won him his Nobel Prize in 1921: "For services to theoretical physics and especially for the discovery of the law of the photoelectric effect." The Nobel committee had waited patiently for experimental confirmation of special relativity; however none was forthcoming until the time dilation experiments of Ives and Stilwell (1938), (1941) and Rossi and Hall (1941).

Papers

1. Photoelectric effect

The paper, "On a Heuristic Viewpoint Concerning the Production and Transformation of Light", proposed the idea of energy quanta. This idea, motivated by Max Planck's earlier derivation of the law of black body radiation, assumes that luminous energy can be absorbed or emitted only in discrete amounts, called quanta. Einstein states,

Energy, during the propagation of a ray of light, is not continuously distributed over steadily increasing spaces, but it consists of a finite number of energy quanta localised at points in space, moving without dividing and capable of being absorbed or generated only as entities.

In explaining the photoelectric effect, the hypothesis that energy consists of discrete packets, as Einstein illustrates, can be directly applied to black bodies, as well.

The idea of light quanta contradicts the wave theory of light that follows naturally from James Clerk Maxwell's equations for electromagnetic behaviour and, more generally, the assumption of infinite divisibility of energy in physical systems.

A profound formal difference exists between the theoretical concepts that physicists have formed about gases and other ponderable bodies, and Maxwell's theory of electromagnetic processes in so-called empty space. While we consider the state of a body to be completely determined by the positions and velocities of an indeed very large yet finite number of atoms and electrons, we make use of continuous spatial functions to determine the electromagnetic state of a volume of space, so that a finite number of quantities cannot be considered as sufficient for the complete determination of the electromagnetic state of space.

This leads to contradictions when applied to the phenomena of emission and transformation of light.

According to the view that the incident light consists of energy quanta, the production of cathode rays by light can be conceived in the following way. The body's surface layer is penetrated by energy quanta whose energy is converted at least partially into kinetic energy of the electrons. The simplest conception is that a light quantum transfers its entire energy to a single electron.

Einstein noted that the photoelectric effect depended on the wavelength, and hence the frequency of the light. At too low a frequency, even intense light produced no electrons. However, once a certain frequency was reached, even low intensity light produced electrons. He compared this to Planck's hypothesis that light could be emitted only in packets of energy given by *hf*, where *h* is Planck's constant and *f* is the frequency. He then postulated that light travels in packets whose energy depends on the frequency, and therefore only light above a certain frequency would bring sufficient energy to liberate an electron.

Even after experiments confirmed that Einstein's equations for the photoelectric effect were accurate, his explanation was not universally accepted. Niels Bohr, in his 1922 Nobel address, stated, "The hypothesis of light-quanta is not able to throw light on the nature of radiation."

By 1921, when Einstein was awarded the Nobel Prize and his work on photoelectricity was mentioned by name in the award citation, some physicists accepted that the equation $(hf = \Phi + E_k)$ was correct and light quanta were possible. In 1923, Arthur Compton's X-ray scattering experiment helped more of the scientific community to accept this formula. The theory of light quanta was a strong indicator of wave-particle duality, a fundamental principle of quantum mechanics. A complete picture of the theory of photoelectricity was realized after the maturity of quantum mechanics.

2. Brownian motion

The article "Über die von der molekularkinetischen Theorie der Wärme geforderte Bewegung von in ruhenden

Flüssigkeiten suspendierten Teilchen" ("On the Motion of Small Particles Suspended in a Stationary Liquid, as Required by the Molecular Kinetic Theory of Heat") delineated a stochastic model of Brownian motion.

In this paper it will be shown that, according to the molecular kinetic theory of heat, bodies of a microscopically visible size suspended in liquids must, as a result of thermal molecular motions, perform motions of such magnitudes that they can be easily observed with a microscope. It is possible that the motions to be discussed here are identical with so-called Brownian molecular motion; however, the data available to me on the latter are so imprecise that I could not form a judgment on the question ...

Brownian motion generates expressions for the root mean square displacement of particles. Using the kinetic theory of fluids, which at the time was controversial, the article established the phenomenon, which was lacking a satisfactory explanation even decades after the first observation, provided empirical evidence for the reality of the atom. It also lent credence to statistical mechanics, which had been controversial at that time, as well. Before this paper, atoms were recognized as a useful concept, but physicists and chemists debated whether atoms were real entities. Einstein's statistical discussion of atomic behaviour gave experimentalists a way to count atoms by looking through an ordinary microscope. Wilhelm Ostwald, one of the leaders of the anti-atom school, later told Arnold Sommerfeld that he had been convinced of the existence of atoms by Einstein's complete explanation of Brownian motion.

3. Special relativity

Einstein's "Zur Elektrodynamik bewegter Körper" ("On the Electrodynamics of Moving Bodies"), his third paper that year, was published on June 30. It reconciles Maxwell's equations for electricity and magnetism with the laws of mechanics, by introducing major changes to mechanics close to the speed of light. This later became known as Einstein's special theory of relativity.

The paper mentions the name of only five other scientists, Isaac Newton, James Clerk Maxwell, Heinrich Hertz, Christian Doppler, and Hendrik Lorentz. It does not have any references to any other publications. Many of the ideas had already been published by others, as detailed in History of special relativity. However, Einstein's paper introduces a new theory of time, distance, mass, and energy that was consistent with electromagnetism, but omitted the force of gravity.

At the time, it was known that Maxwell's equations, when applied to moving bodies, led to asymmetries, and that it had not been possible to discover any motion of the Earth relative to the 'light medium'. Einstein puts forward two postulates to explain these observations. First, he applies the classic principle of relativity, which states that the laws of physics remain the same for any non-accelerating frame of reference (called an inertial reference frame), to the laws of electrodynamics and optics as well as mechanics. In the second postulate, Einstein proposes that the speed of light has the same value in all inertial frames of reference, independent of the state of motion of the emitting body.

Special relativity is thus consistent with the result of the Michelson-Morley experiment, which had not detected a medium of conductance (or aether) for light waves unlike other known waves that require a medium (such as water or air). Einstein states,

... the unsuccessful attempts to discover any motion of the earth relatively to the "light medium," suggest that the phenomena of electrodynamics as well as of mechanics possess no properties corresponding to the idea of absolute rest.

The speed of light is fixed, and thus not relative to the movement of the observer. This was impossible under Newtonian classical mechanics. Einstein argues,

... the same laws of electrodynamics and optics will be valid for all frames of reference for which the equations of mechanics hold good. We will raise this conjecture (the purport of which will hereafter be called the "Principle of Relativity") to the status of a postulate, and also introduce another postulate, which is only apparently irreconcilable with the former, namely, that light is always propagated in empty space with a definite velocity c which is independent of the state of motion of the emitting body. These two postulates suffice for the attainment of a simple and consistent theory of the electrodynamics of moving bodies based on

Maxwell's theory for stationary bodies. The introduction of a "luminiferous ether" will prove to be superfluous in as much as the view here to be developed will not require an "absolutely stationary space" provided with special properties, nor assign a velocity-vector to a point of the empty space in which electromagnetic processes take place.

The theory is based-like all electrodynamics-on the kinematics of the rigid body, since the assertions of any such theory have to do with the relationships between rigid bodies (systems of co-ordinates), clocks, and electromagnetic processes. Insufficient consideration of this circumstance lies at the root of the difficulties which the electrodynamics of moving bodies at present encounters.

It had previously been conjectured, by George FitzGerald in 1894 and by Lorentz in 1895, independent of each other, that the Michelson-Morley result could be accounted for if moving bodies were contracted in the direction of their motion. Some of the paper's core equations, the Lorentz transforms, had been published by Joseph Larmor (1897, 1900), Hendrik Lorentz (1899, 1903, 1904) and Henri Poincaré (1905), in a development of Lorentz's 1904 paper. Einstein revealed the underlying causes for this geometrical oddity, which differed from the explanations given by FitzGerald, Larmor, and Lorentz, but were similar in many respects to the reasons given by Poincaré (1905).

His explanation arises from two axioms. First, Galileo's idea that the laws of nature should be the same for all observers that move with constant speed relative to each other. Einstein writes,

The laws by which the states of physical systems undergo change are not affected, whether these changes of state be referred to the one or the other of two systems of co-ordinates in uniform translatory motion.

The second is the rule that the speed of light is the same for every observer.

Any ray of light moves in the "stationary" system of co-ordinates with the determined velocity c, whether the ray be emitted by a stationary or by a moving body.

The theory, now called the special theory of relativity, distinguishes it from his later general theory of relativity, which considers all observers to be equivalent. Special relativity gained widespread acceptance remarkably quickly, confirming Einstein's comment that it had been "ripe for discovery" in 1905. Acknowledging the role of Max Planck in the early dissemination of his ideas, Einstein wrote in 1913 "The attention that this theory so quickly received from colleagues is surely to be ascribed in large part to the resoluteness and warmth with which he [Planck] intervened for this theory". In addition, the improved mathematical formulation of the theory by Hermann Minkowski in 1907 was influential in gaining acceptance for the theory. Also, and most importantly, the theory was supported by an ever-increasing body of confirmatory experimental evidence.

4. Matter and energy equivalence

On September 27 *Annalen der Physik* published a fourth paper, "Ist die Trägheit eines Körpers von seinem Energieinhalt abhängig?" ("Does the Inertia of a Body Depend Upon Its Energy Content?"), in which Einstein developed an argument for arguably the most famous equation in the field of physics: $E = mc^2$. Einstein considered the equivalency equation to be of paramount importance because it showed that a massive particle possesses an energy, the "rest energy", distinct from its classical kinetic and potential energies.

The paper is based on James Clerk Maxwell's and Heinrich Rudolf Hertz's investigations and, in addition, the axioms of relativity, as Einstein states,

The results of the previous investigation lead to a very interesting conclusion, which is here to be deduced.

The previous investigation was based "on the Maxwell-Hertz equations for empty space, together with the Maxwellian expression for the electromagnetic energy of space ... "

The laws by which the states of physical systems alter are independent of the alternative, to which of two systems of coordinates, in uniform motion of parallel translation relatively to each other, these alterations of state are referred (principle of relativity).

The equation sets forth that energy of a body at rest (E) equals its mass (m) times the speed of light (c) squared, or $E = mc^2$.

If a body gives off the energy L *in the form of radiation, its mass diminishes by L/c². The fact that the energy withdrawn from the body becomes energy of radiation evidently makes no difference, so that we are led to the more general conclusion that.*

The mass of a body is a measure of its energy-content; if the energy changes by L, the mass changes in the same sense by L/9 × 1020, the energy being measured in ergs, and the mass in grammes.

If the theory corresponds to the facts, radiation conveys inertia between the emitting and absorbing bodies.

The mass-energy relation can be used to predict how much energy will be released or consumed by nuclear reactions; one simply measures the mass of all constituents and products and multiplies the difference by c2. The result shows how much energy will be released or consumed, usually in the form of light or heat. When applied to certain nuclear reactions, the equation shows that an extraordinarily large amount of energy will be released, much larger than in the combustion of chemical explosives, where the mass difference is hardly measurable at all. This explains why nuclear weapons produce such phenomenal amounts of energy, as they release binding energy during nuclear fission and nuclear fusion, and also convert a much larger portion of subatomic mass to energy.

Commemoration

The International Union of Pure and Applied Physics (IUPAP) resolved to commemorate the 100th year of the publication of Einstein's extensive work in 1905 as the 'World Year of Physics 2005'. This was subsequently endorsed by both the United Nations and the United States Congress.

Thermodynamic Fluctuations and Statistical Physics

Einstein's earliest papers were concerned with thermodynamics. He wrote a paper establishing a thermodynamic identity in 1902, and a few other papers which attempted to interpret phenomena from a statistical atomic point of view.

His research in 1903 and 1904 was mainly concerned with the effect of finite atomic size on diffusion phenomena. As in Maxwell's work, the finite nonzero size of atoms leads to effects which can be observed. This research, and the thermodynamic identity, were well within the mainstream of physics in his time. They would eventually form the content of his PhD thesis.

His first major result in this field was the theory of thermodynamic fluctuations. When in equilibrium, a system has a maximum entropy and according to the statistical interpretation, it can fluctuate a little bit. Einstein pointed out that the statistical fluctuations of a macroscopic object, like a mirror suspended on spring, would be completely determined by the second derivative of the entropy with respect to the position of the mirror. This makes a connection between microscopic and macroscopic objects.

Searching for ways to test this relation, his great breakthrough came in 1905. The theory of fluctuations, he realized, would have a visible effect for an object which could move around freely. Such an object would have a velocity which is random, and would move around randomly, just like an individual atom. The average kinetic energy of the object would be $k_B T$, and the time decay of the fluctuations would be entirely determined by the law of friction.

The law of friction for a small ball in a viscous fluid like water was discovered by George Stokes. He showed that for small velocities, the friction force would be proportional to the velocity, and to the radius of the particle. This relation could be used to calculate how far a small ball in water would travel due to its random thermal motion, and Einstein noted that such a ball, of size about a micron, would travel about a few microns per second. This motion could be easily observed with a microscope. Such a motion had already been observed with a microscope by a Botanist named Brown, and had been called Brownian motion. Einstein was able to identify this motion with the motion predicted by his theory. Since the fluctuations which give rise to Brownian motion are just the same as the fluctuations of the velocities of atoms, measuring the precise amount of Brownian motion using Einstein's theory would show that Boltzmann's constant is nonzero. It would measure Avogadro's number.

These experiments were carried out a few years later, and gave a rough estimate of Avogadro's number consistent with the more accurate estimates due to Max Planck's theory of blackbody light, and Robert Millikan's measurement of the charge of the electron. Unlike the other methods, Einstein's required very few theoretical assumptions or new physics, since it was directly measuring atomic motion on visible grains.

Einstein's theory of Brownian motion was the first paper in the field of statistical physics. It established that thermodynamic fluctuations were related to dissipation. This was shown by Einstein to be true for time-independent fluctuations, but in the Brownian motion paper he showed that dynamical relaxation rates calculated from classical mechanics could be used as statistical relaxation rates to derive dynamical diffusion laws. These relations are known as Einstein relations.

The theory of Brownian motion was the least revolutionary of Einstein's Annus mirabilis papers, but it had an important role in securing the acceptance of the atomic theory by physicists.

Statistical physics

Statistical physics is the area of physics that uses methods of probability theory and statistics, and particularly the mathematical tools for dealing with large populations, in solving physical problems. It can describe a wide variety of fields with an inherently stochastic nature. Examples include problems involving nuclear reactions, and topics in the fields of biology, chemistry, neurology and even some social sciences such as sociology.

Historically, one of the first topics in physics where statistical methods were applied was the field of mechanics, which is concerned with the motion of particles or objects when subjected to a force. Statistical mechanics provides a framework for relating the microscopic properties of individual atoms and molecules to the macroscopic or bulk properties of materials that can be observed in everyday life, therefore explaining thermodynamics as a natural result of statistics and mechanics (classical and quantum) at the microscopic level. Because of this history, the term "statistical physics" is therefore sometimes used as a synonym for statistical mechanics or statistical thermodynamics, rather than in the wider sense considered in this article.

A statistical approach can work well in classical systems when the number of degrees of freedom (and so the number of variables) is so large that exact solution is not possible, or not really useful. Statistical mechanics can also describe work in non-linear dynamics, chaos theory, thermal physics, fluid dynamics (particularly at high Knudsen numbers), or plasma physics.

Although some problems in statistical physics can be solved analytically using approximations and expansions, most current research utilizes the large processing power of modern computers to simulate or approximate solutions. A common approach to statistical problems is to use a Monte Carlo simulation to yield insight into the dynamics of a complex system.

Thought Experiments and A-Priori Physical Principles

Einstein's thinking underwent a transformation in 1905. He had come to understand that quantum properties of light mean that Maxwell's equations were only an approximation. He knew that new laws would have to replace these, but he did not know how to go about finding those laws. He felt that guessing formal relations would not go anywhere.

So he decided to focus on a-priori principles instead, which are statements about physical laws which can be understood to hold in a very broad sense even in domains where they have not yet been shown to apply. A well accepted example of an a-priori principle is rotational invariance. If a new force is discovered in physics, it is assumed to be rotationally invariant almost automatically, without thought. Einstein sought new principles of this sort, to guide the production of physical ideas. Once enough principles are found, then the new physics will be the simplest theory consistent with the principles and with previously known laws.

The first general a-priori principle he found was the principle of relativity, that uniform motion is indistinguishable from rest. This was understood by Hermann Minkowski to be a generalization of rotational invariance from space to space-time. Other principles postulated by Einstein and later vindicated, are the principle of equivalence and the principle of adiabatic invariance of the quantum number. Another of Einstein's general principles, Mach's principle is fiercely debated, and whether it holds in our world or not is still not definitively established.

The use of a-priori principles is a distinctive unique signature of Einstein's early work, which has become a standard tool in modern theoretical physics.

Thought experiment

A thought experiment, sometimes called by the German name gedankenexperiment, is a proposal for an experiment that would test or illuminate a hypothesis or theory.

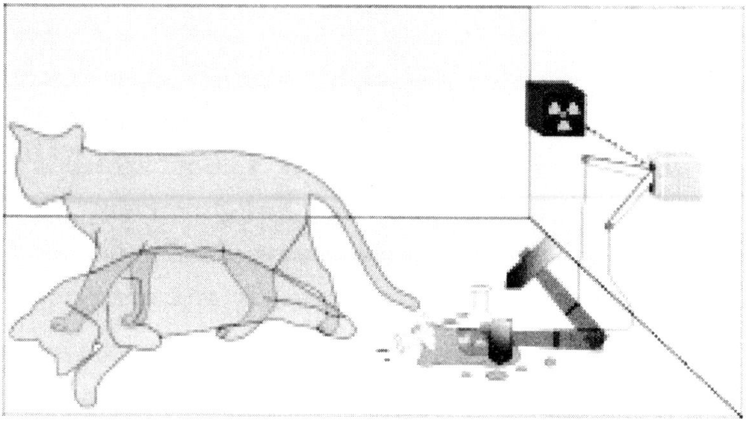

In a famous example, Schrödinger's Cat (1935), presents a cat that might be alive or dead, depending on an earlier random event. It illustrates the problem of the Copenhagen interpretation applied to everyday objects.

Given the structure of the proposed experiment, it may or may not be possible to actually perform the experiment and, in the case that it is possible for the experiment to be performed, there may be no intention of any kind to actually perform the experiment in question. The common goal of a thought experiment is to explore the potential consequences of the principle in question.

Famous examples of *thought experiments* include Schrödinger's cat, illustrating quantum indeterminacy through the manipulation of a perfectly sealed environment and a tiny bit of radioactive substance, and Maxwell's demon, in which a supernatural being is instructed to attempt to violate the second law of thermodynamics.

Overview

As the contemporary philosopher Martin Cohen puts it, "much of modern physics is built not upon measurement but on thought experimentation". As Cohen argues, the Renaissance period and the Enlightenment were characterized by breakthroughs in ways of seeing the world, not merely by new methods (and tools) for 'measuring' it.

Thus it is that perhaps the key experiment in the history of modern science, again toppling the lofty but inaccurate view of Aristotle, is Galileo's demonstration that falling objects must fall at the same rate regardless of their masses. This is widely thought to have been a straightforward physical demonstration, involving climbing up the Leaning Tower of Pisa and dropping two heavy weights off it, whereas in fact, it was clearly a logical demonstration, using the 'thought experiment' technique. The 'experiment' is described by Galileo in *Discorsi e dimostrazioni matematiche* (1628) (literally, 'Mathematical Discourses and Demonstrations') thus:

Salviati. *If then we take two bodies whose natural speeds are different, it is clear that on uniting the two, the more rapid one will be partly retarded by the slower, and the slower will be somewhat hastened by the swifter. Do you not agree with me in this opinion?*

Simplicio. *You are unquestionably right.*

Salviati. *But if this is true, and if a large stone moves with a speed of, say, eight while a smaller moves with a speed of four, then when they are united, the system will move with a speed less than eight; but the two stones when tied together make a stone larger than that which before moved with a speed of eight. Hence the heavier body moves with less speed than the lighter; an effect which is contrary to your supposition. Thus you see how, from your assumption that the heavier body moves more rapidly than the lighter one, I infer that the heavier body moves more slowly.*

Although the extract does not convey the elegance and power of the 'demonstration' terribly well, it is clear that it is a 'thought' experiment, rather than a practical one. Strange then, as Cohen says, that philosophers and scientists alike refuse to acknowledge either Galileo in particular, or the thought experiment technique in general for its pivotal role in both science and philosophy. (The exception proves the rule — the iconoclastic philosopher of science, Paul Feyerabend, has also observed this methodological prejudice.)

Instead, many philosophers prefer to consider '*Thought experiments*' to be merely the use of a hypothetical scenario to help understand the way things actually are.

Different kinds of thought experiments

There are different kinds of *thought experiments*. All *thought experiments*, however, employ a methodology that is a priori, rather than empirical, in that they do not proceed by observation or physical experiment.

Thought experiments have been used in a variety of fields, including philosophy, law, physics, and mathematics. In philosophy, they have been used at least since classical antiquity, some pre-dating Socrates. In law, they were well-known to Roman lawyers quoted in the Digest. In physics and other sciences, notable thought experiments date from the 19th and especially the 20th century, but examples can be found at least as early as Galileo.

Origins and use of the literal term "thought experiment"

Witt-Hansen established that Hans Christian Ørsted was the first to use the Latin-German mixed term

Gedankenexperiment (lit. experiment conducted in the thoughts) circa 1812. Ørsted was also the first to use its entirely German equivalent, *Gedankenversuch*, in 1820.

Much later, Ernst Mach used the term *Gedankenexperiment* in a different way to exclusively denote the imaginary conduct of a *real* experiment that would be subsequently performed as a *real physical experiment* by his students (thus the contrast between physical and mental experimentation) with Mach asking his students to provide him with explanations whenever it happened that the results from their subsequent, real, physical experiment had differed from those of their prior, imaginary experiment.

The English term *thought experiment* was coined (as a calque) from Mach's *Gedankenexperiment*, and it first appeared in the 1897 English translation of one of Mach's papers. Prior to its emergence, the activity of posing hypothetical questions that employed subjunctive reasoning had existed for a very long time (for both scientists and philosophers). However, people had no way of categorizing it or speaking about it. This helps to explain the extremely wide and diverse range of the application of the term "thought experiment" once it had been introduced into English.

Thought experimentation in general

In its broadest usage, thought experimentation is the process of employing imaginary situations to help us understand the way things really are (or, in the case of Herman Kahn's "scenarios", understand something about something in the future). The understanding comes through reflection upon this imaginary situation. Thought experimentation is a priori, rather than an empirical process, in that the experiments are conducted within the imagination (i.e., Brown's (1993) "laboratory of the mind"), and never in fact.

Thought experiments, which are well-structured, well-defined hypothetical questions that employ subjunctive reasoning (irrealis moods) -- "What might happen (or, what might have happened) if . . . " -- have been used to pose questions in philosophy at least since Greek antiquity, some pre-dating Socrates. In physics and other sciences many famous *thought experiments* date from the 19th and especially the 20th Century, but examples can be found at least as early as Galileo.

Thought experiments have been used in philosophy, physics, and other fields (such as cognitive psychology, history, political science, economics, social psychology, law, organizational studies, marketing, and epidemiology). In law, the synonym "hypothetical" is frequently used for such experiments.

Regardless of their intended goal, all thought experiments display a patterned way of thinking that is designed to allow us to explain, predict and control events in a better and more productive way.

The theoretical consequences of thought experimentation

In terms of their theoretical consequences, *thought experiments* generally:

- challenge (or, even, refute) a prevailing theory, often involving the device known as reductio ad absurdum, (as in Galileo's original argument, a proof by contradiction),
- confirm a prevailing theory,
- establish a new theory, or
- simultaneously refute a prevailing theory and establish a new theory through a process of mutual exclusion.

The practical application of thought experimentation

Thought experiments often introduce interesting, important and valuable new perspectives on old mysteries and old questions; yet, although they may make old questions irrelevant, they may also create new questions that are not easy to answer.

In terms of their practical application, *thought experiments* are generally created in order to:

- challenge the prevailing status quo (which includes activities such as correcting misinformation (or misapprehension), identify flaws in the argument(s) presented, to preserve (for the long-term) objectively established fact, and to refute specific assertions that some particular thing is permissible, forbidden, known, believed, possible, or necessary);

- extrapolate beyond (or interpolate within) the boundaries of already established fact;
- predict and forecast the (otherwise) indefinite and unknowable future;
- explain the past;
- the retrodiction, postdiction and postcasting of the (otherwise) indefinite and unknowable past;
- facilitate decision making, choice and strategy selection;
- solve problems, and generate ideas;
- move current (often insoluble) problems into another, more helpful and more productive problem space (e.g., see functional fixedness);
- attribute causation, preventability, blame and responsibility for specific outcomes;
- assess culpability and compensatory damages in social and legal contexts;
- ensure the repeat of past success; or
- examine the extent to which past events might have occurred differently.
- ensure the (future) avoidance of past failures.

Thought experimentation in science

Scientists tend to use thought experiments in the form of imaginary, "proxy" experiments which they conduct prior to a real, "physical" experiment (Ernst Mach always argued that these *gedankenexperiments* were "a necessary precondition for physical experiment"). In these cases, the result of the "proxy" experiment will often be so clear that there will be no need to conduct a physical experiment at all.

Scientists also use thought experiments when particular physical experiments are impossible to conduct (Carl Gustav Hempel labeled these sorts of experiment "*theoretical experiments-in-imagination*"), such as Einstein's thought experiment of chasing a light beam, leading to Special Relativity. This is a unique use of a scientific thought experiment, in that it was never carried out, but led to a successful theory, proven by other empirical means.

Relation to real experiments

The relation to *real experiments* can be quite complex, as can be seen again from an example going back to Albert Einstein. In 1935, with two co-workers, he published a famous paper on a newly-created subject called later the EPR effect (EPR paradox). In this paper, starting from certain philosophical assumptions, on the basis of a rigorous analysis of a certain, complicated, but in the meantime realizable model, he came to the conclusion that *quantum mechanics should be rejected as "incomplete"*. There were of course influential people, e.g.

Niels Bohr, who refuted Einstein's analysis immediately. However it took decades, until the error in Einstein's paper was located by a real experiment. This means that finally, after decades, there was a decision. The outcome: there was no error, neither in Einstein's analysis nor in his model, but the above-mentioned philosophical starting assumptions were falsified (e.g. by the optical *real experiments* of Alain Aspect). This was only possible after the Bell inequalities had been published in 1964, another rigorous theoretical paper.

Thus *thought experiments* belong to a theoretical discipline, usually to theoretical physics, but often to theoretical philosophy. In any case, it must be distinguished from a real experiment, which belongs naturally to the experimental discipline and has "the final decision on *true* or *not true*", at least in physics.

Causal reasoning in thought experiments

Generally speaking, there are seven types of thought experiments in which one reasons from causes to effects, or effects to causes:

Prefactual thought experiments

Prefactual (before the fact) thought experiments speculate on possible future outcomes, given the present, and ask "What will be the outcome if event E occurs?"

Counterfactual thought experiments

Counterfactual *(contrary to established fact) thought experiments* speculate on the possible outcomes of a different past; and ask "What might have happened if A had happened instead of B?" (e.g., "If Isaac Newton and Gottfried Leibniz *had* cooperated with each other, what would mathematics look like today?")

Semifactual thought experiments

Semifactual thought experiments speculate on the extent to which things might have remained the same, despite there being a different past; and asks the question Even though *X* happened instead of *E*, would *Y* have still occurred? (e.g., Even if the goalie had moved left, rather than right, could he have intercepted a ball that was travelling at such a speed?)

Semifactual speculations are an important part of clinical medicine.

Prediction, forecasting and nowcasting

The activities of *prediction, forecasting* and *nowcasting* attempt to project the circumstances of the present into the future (the only difference between these identically patterned activities being the distance of their speculated future from the present).

Hindcasting

The activity of *hindcasting* involves running a forecast model after an event has happened in order to test whether the model's simulation is valid.

Retrodiction (or postdiction)

The activity of *retrodiction* (or *postdiction*) involves moving backwards in time, step-by-step, in as many stages as are considered necessary, from the present into the speculated past, in order to establish the ultimate cause of a specific event (e.g., Reverse engineering and Forensics).

Backcasting

The activity of backcasting involves establishing the description of a very definite and very specific future situation. It then involves an imaginary moving backwards in time, step-by-step, in as many stages as are considered necessary, from the future to the present, in order to reveal the mechanism through which that particular specified future could be attained from the present.

It is important to recognize that a major difficulty with all types of thought experiment, and particularly with *counterfactual thought experiments*, is that there are no formally accepted criteria for accurately measuring the risk of either Type I errors (False positive) or *Type II errors* (False negative) in the choice of a potential causative factor.

Thought experiments in philosophy

Whereas thought experiments in physics are intended to give us a priori knowledge of the natural world, philosophy attempts to produce a priori knowledge of our concepts:

[Philosophical and scientific] investigations differ both in their methods (the former is a priori, and the latter a posteriori) and in the metaphysical status of their results (the former yields facts that are metaphysically necessary and the latter yields facts that are metaphysically contingent). Yet the two types of

investigations resemble each other in that both, if successful, uncover new facts, and these facts, although expressed in language, are generally not about language (except for investigations in such specialized areas as philosophy of language and empirical linguistics).

In philosophy, a thought experiment typically presents an imagined scenario with the intention of eliciting an intuitive response about the way things are in the thought experiment. (Philosophers might also supplement their *thought experiments* with theoretical reasoning designed to support the desired intuitive response.) The scenario will typically be designed to target a particular philosophical notion, such as morality, or the nature of the mind or linguistic reference. The intuitive response to the imagined scenario is supposed to tell us about the nature of that notion in any scenario, real or imagined.

For example, a thought experiment might present a situation in which an agent intentionally kills an innocent for the benefit of others. Here, the relevant question is whether the action is moral or not, but more broadly whether a moral theory is correct that says morality is determined solely by an action's consequences. John Searle imagines a man in a locked room who receives written sentences in Chinese, and returns written sentences in Chinese, according to a sophisticated instruction manual. Here, the relevant question is whether or not the man understands Chinese, but more broadly, whether a functionalist theory of mind is correct.

It is generally hoped that there is universal agreement about the intuitions that a thought experiment elicits. (Hence, in assessing their own *thought experiments*, philosophers may appeal to "what we should say," or some such locution.) A successful thought experiment will be one in which intuitions about it are widely shared. But often, philosophers differ in their intuitions about the scenario.

Other philosophical uses of imagined scenarios arguably are thought experiments also. In one use of scenarios, philosophers might imagine persons in a particular situation (maybe ourselves), and ask what they would do.

For example, John Rawls asks us to imagine a group of persons in a situation where they know nothing about themselves, and are charged with devising a social or political organization. The use of the state of nature to imagine the origins of government, as by Thomas Hobbes and John Locke, may also be considered a thought experiment. Similarly, Nietzsche, in On the Genealogy of Morals, speculated about the historical development of Judeo-Christian morality, with the intent of questioning its legitimacy.

One of the earliest known *thought experiments* was Avicenna's "Floating Man" thought experiment in the 11th century. He asked his readers to imagine themselves suspended in the air isolated from all sensations in order to demonstrate human self-awareness and self-consciousness, and the substantiality of the soul.

Philosophical thought experiments and possibility

The scenario presented in a thought experiment must be possible in some sense. In many *thought experiments*, the scenario would be nomologically possible, or possible according to the laws of nature. John Searle's Chinese Room is nomologically possible.

Some *thought experiments* present scenarios that are not nomologically possible. In his Twin Earth thought experiment, Hilary Putnam asks us to imagine a scenario in which there is a substance with all of the observable properties of water (e.g., taste, colour, boiling point), but which is chemically different from water. It has been argued that this thought experiment is not nomologically possible, although it may be possible in some other sense, such as metaphysical possibility. It is debatable whether the nomological impossibility of a thought experiment renders intuitions about it moot.

In some cases, the hypothetical scenario might be considered metaphysically impossible, or impossible in any sense at all. David Chalmers says that we can imagine that there are zombies, or persons who are physically identical to us in every way but who lack consciousness. This is supposed to show that physicalism is false. However, some argue that zombies are inconceivable: we can no more imagine a zombie than we can imagine that 1+1=3. Others have claimed that the conceivability of a scenario may not entail its possibility.

Other criticisms of philosophical thought experiments

The use of *thought experiments* in philosophy has received other criticisms, especially in the philosophy of mind. Daniel Dennett has derisively referred to certain types of *thought experiments* such as the Chinese Room experiment as "intuition pumps", claiming they are simply thinly veiled appeals to intuition which fail when carefully analyzed. Another criticism that has been voiced is that some science fiction-type *thought experiments* are too wild to yield clear intuitions, or that any resulting intuitions could not possibly pertain to the real world. Another criticism is that philosophers have used *thought experiments* (and other a priori methods) in areas where empirical science should be the primary method of discovery, as for example, with issues about the mind.

Famous thought experiments

Physics

Thought experiments are popular in physics and include:

- Bell's spaceship paradox (special relativity)
- Brownian ratchet (Richard Feynman's "perpetual motion" machine that does not violate the second law and does no work at thermal equilibrium)
- Bucket argument – argues that space is absolute, not relational
- Double-slit experiment (quantum mechanics)

- Elitzur-Vaidman bomb-tester (quantum mechanics)
- Einstein's box
- EPR paradox (quantum mechanics) (forms of this have actually been performed)
- Feynman sprinkler (classical mechanics)
- Galileo's ship (classical relativity principle) 1632
- Galileo's Leaning Tower of Pisa experiment (rebuttal of Aristotelian Gravity)
- GHZ experiment (quantum mechanics)
- Heisenberg's microscope (quantum mechanics)
- Kepler's Dream (change of point of view as support for the Copernican hypothesis)
- Ladder paradox (special relativity)
- Laplace's demon
- Maxwell's demon (thermodynamics) 1871
- Monkey and the Hunter, The (gravitation)
- Moving magnet and conductor problem
- Newton's cannonball (Newton's laws of motion)
- Popper's experiment (quantum mechanics)
- Quantum pseudo telepathy (quantum mechanics)
- Quantum suicide (quantum mechanics)
- Schrödinger's cat (quantum mechanics)

- Sticky bead argument (general relativity)
- Renninger negative-result experiment (quantum mechanics)
- Twin paradox (special relativity)
- Wheeler's delayed choice experiment (quantum mechanics)
- Wigner's friend (quantum mechanics)
- Wittgenstein's rod (engineering mechanics) – an exercise in visualization

Philosophy

The field of philosophy makes extensive use of thought experiments:

- Artificial brain
- *Bellum omnium contra omnes*
- Big Book (ethics)
- Brain-in-a-vat (epistemology, philosophy of mind)
- Brainstorm machine
- Buridan's ass
- Changing places (reflexive monism, philosophy of mind)
- China brain (physicalism, philosophy of mind)
- Chinese room (philosophy of mind, artificial intelligence, cognitive science)

- Coherence (philosophical gambling strategy)
- Robinson's rotating/still spheres (metaphysics)
- gettier problem(epistomology)
- Hilary Putnam's Twin Earth thought experiment in the philosophy of language and philosophy of mind
- How many men? (taxation as theft)
- Inverted spectrum
- Kavka's toxin puzzle
- Mary's room (philosophy of mind)
- Molyneux's Problem (admittedly, this oscillated between empirical and a-priori assessment)
- Newcomb's paradox
- Original position (politics)
- Philosophical zombie (philosophy of mind, artificial intelligence, cognitive science)
- Plank of Carneades
- Ship of Theseus, The (concept of identity)
- Simulated reality (philosophy, computer science, cognitive science)
- Social contract theories
- Strawson's auditory world
- Survival lottery, The Ethics

- Swamp man (personal identity, philosophy of mind)
- Shoemaker's "*Time Without Change*" (metaphysics)
- Ticking time bomb scenario (ethics)
- Teleport (metaphysics)
- time without change (metaphysics)
- Trolley problem (ethics)
- The Violinist (ethics)
- Utility monster (ethics)

Zeno's paradoxes (classical Greek problems of the infinite)

Mathematics

- Balls and vase problem (infinity and cardinality)
- Gabriel's Horn (infinity)
- Infinite monkey theorem (probability)
- Lottery paradox (probability)
- Sleeping beauty paradox (probability)
- Wittgenstein's rod (geometry)

Biology

- Levinthal paradox

Computer science

- Halting problem (limits of computability)
- Turing machine (limits of computability)

- Two Generals' Problem
- Dining Philosophers (computer science)

Miscellaneous

- Buttered cat paradox
- Braitenberg vehicles (robotics, neural control and sensing systems) (some have actually been built)
- Doomsday argument (anthropic principle)
- Dyson sphere
- The Lady, or the Tiger? (human nature) The Planiverse

Special Relativity

Electrodynamics of moving bodies

In September 1905 (received June 30), Albert Einstein published his annus mirabilis paper on what is now called Special Relativity. Einstein's paper includes a fundamental new definition of space and time (all time and space coordinates in all reference frames are equal, so there is no "true" or "apparent" time) and the abolition of the aether.

Because of his axiomatic method, Einstein was able to derive *all results* of his predecessors and in addition the formula for the Relativistic Doppler effect and Relativistic aberration — on a few pages, while his predecessors needed many years of long, complicated work to arrive at the same mathematical formalism. Einstein identified two fundamental principles, the Principle of Relativity and the *Principle of the Constancy of Light*, motivated, respectively, by the lack of evidence for the luminiferous ether and Maxwell's theory of electromagnetism but not, contrary to widespread belief, the null result of the Michelson-Morley experiment. Taken together (along with a few other tacit assumptions such as isotropy and homogeneity of space), these two postulates lead uniquely to the mathematics of Lorentz's electrodynamics and special relativity. Lorentz and Poincaré had also adopted these same principles, as necessary to achieve their final results, but didn't recognize that they were also sufficient, and hence that they obviated all the other assumptions underlying Lorentz's initial derivations.

It's notable that Einstein's paper contains no references to other papers. However, many historians of science like Holton, Miller and Stachel, have tried to find out possible influences on Einstein. Einstein himself stated that his thinking was influenced by the empiricist philosophers David Hume and Ernst Mach. Regarding the Relativity Principle, the moving magnet and conductor problem (possibly after reading a book of August Föppl) and the various negative aether drift experiments were important for him to accept that principle — but he denied any significant influence of the most important experiment: the Michelson-Morley experiment. Other possible sources are Poincaré's *Science and Hypothesis*, where he described the Principle of Relativity and which was read by Einstein in 1904, and the writings of Max Abraham, from whom he borrowed the terms "Maxwell-Hertz equations" and "longitudinal and transverse mass".

Regarding his views on Electrodynamics and the *Principle of the Constancy of Light*, Einstein himself stated that Lorentz's theory of 1895 (or the Maxwell-Lorentz electrodynamics) and also the Fizeau experiment had considerable influence on his thinking. He said in 1909 and 1912 that he borrowed that principle from Lorentz's stationary ether (which implies validity of Maxwell's equations and the constancy of light in the ether frame), but he recognized that this principle together with the principle of relativity makes the ether useless. As he wrote in 1907 and in later papers, the apparent contradiction between those principles can be solved if it is realized that Lorentz's local time is not an auxiliary quantity, but can simply be defined as time and is connected with signal velocity. Before Einstein, also Poincaré developed a similar physical interpretation of local time and noticed the connection to signal velocity, but contrary to Einstein he continued to argue that clocks in the aether show the true *time*, and moving clocks show the apparent time. Eventually, in 1953 Einstein described the advances of his theory (although Poincaré already stated in 1905 that Lorentz invariance is a general condition for any physical theory):

"There is no doubt, that the special theory of relativity, if we regard its development in retrospect, was ripe for discovery in 1905. Lorentz had already recognized that the transformations named after him are essential for the analysis of Maxwell's equations, and Poincaré deepened this insight still further. Concerning myself, I knew only Lorentz's important work of 1895 but not Lorentz's later work, nor the consecutive investigations by Poincaré. In this sense my work of 1905 was independent.The new feature of it was the realization of the fact that the bearing of the Lorentz transformation transcended its connection with Maxwell's equations and was concerned with the nature of space and time in general. A further new result was that the "Lorentz invariance" is a general condition for any physical theory. This was for me of particular importance because I had already previously found that Maxwell's theory did not account for the micro-structure of radiation and could therefore have no general validity."

Mass-energy equivalence

Already in §10 of his paper on electrodynamics, Einstein used the formula

$$E_{kin} = mc^2 \left(\frac{1}{\sqrt{1 - \frac{v^2}{c^2}}} - 1 \right)$$

for the kinetic energy of an electron (similar formulae were already used before Einstein by Wien, Poincaré, Abraham, Lorentz, and Hasenöhrl; see the description above). In elaboration of this, in November 1905 (received September 27) Einstein was the first to suggest that when a material body lost energy (either radiation or heat) of amount E, its mass decreased by the amount E/c^2. So, he solved Poincaré's radiation paradox from 1900. This led to the famous mass-energy equivalence formula: $E = mc^2$. Einstein considered the equivalency equation to be of paramount importance because it showed that a massive particle possesses an energy, the "rest energy", distinct from its classical kinetic and potential energies.

Albert Einstein's 1905 paper on the electrodynamics of moving bodies introduced his theory of special relativity, which showed that the observed independence of the speed of light on the observer's state of motion required fundamental changes to the notion of simultaneity. Consequences of this include the time-space frame of a moving body slowing down and contracting (in the direction of motion) relative to the frame of the observer. This paper also argued that the idea of a luminiferous aether — one of the leading theoretical entities in physics at the time — was superfluous. In his paper on *mass-energy equivalence*, which had previously considered to be distinct concepts, Einstein deduced from his equations of special relativity what has been called the twentieth century's best-known equation: $E = mc^2$. This equation suggests that tiny amounts of mass could be converted into huge amounts of energy and presaged the development of nuclear power. Einstein's 1905 work on relativity remained controversial for many years, but was accepted by leading physicists, starting with Max Planck.

Photons

In physics, a photon is an elementary particle, the quantum of the electromagnetic field and the basic "unit" of light and all other forms of electromagnetic radiation. It is also the force carrier for the electromagnetic force. The effects of this force are easily observable at both the microscopic and macroscopic level, because the photon has no rest mass; this allows for interactions at long distances. Like all elementary particles, photons are governed by quantum mechanics and will exhibit wave-particle duality — they exhibit properties of both waves and particles. For example, a single photon may be refracted by a lens or exhibit wave interference, but also act as a particle giving a definite result when quantitative mass is measured.

The modern concept of the photon was developed gradually by Albert Einstein to explain experimental observations that did not fit the classical wave model of light. In particular, the photon model accounted for the frequency dependence of light's energy, and explained the ability of matter and radiation to be in thermal equilibrium. It also accounted for anomalous observations, including the properties of black body radiation, that other physicists, most notably Max Planck, had sought to explain using *semiclassical models*, in which light is still described by Maxwell's equations, but the material objects that emit and absorb light are quantized. Although these semiclassical models contributed to the development of quantum mechanics, further experiments proved Einstein's hypothesis that *light itself* is quantized; the quanta of light are photons.

In the modern Standard Model of particle physics, photons are described as a necessary consequence of physical laws having a certain symmetry at every point in spacetime. The intrinsic properties of photons, such as charge, mass and spin, are determined by the properties of this gauge symmetry.

The photon concept has led to momentous advances in experimental and theoretical physics, such as lasers, Bose-Einstein condensation, quantum field theory, and the probabilistic interpretation of quantum mechanics. It has been applied to photochemistry, high-resolution microscopy, and measurements of molecular distances. Recently, photons have been studied as elements of quantum computers and for sophisticated applications in optical communication such as quantum cryptography.

In physics, a photon is usually denoted by the symbol γ (the Greek letter gamma). This symbol for the photon probably derives from gamma rays, which were discovered and named in 1900 by Paul Villard and shown to be a form of electromagnetic radiation in 1914 by Ernest Rutherford and Edward Andrade. In chemistry and optical engineering, photons are usually symbolized by $h\nu$, the energy of a photon, where h is Planck's constant and the Greek letter ν (nu) is the photon's frequency. Much less commonly, the photon can be symbolized by hf, where its frequency is denoted by f.

Physical properties

The photon is massless, has no electric charge, and does not decay spontaneously in empty space. A photon has two possible polarization (disambiguation) states and is described by exactly three continuous parameters: the components of its wave vector, which determine its wavelength λ and its direction of propagation. The photon is the gauge boson for electromagnetism, and therefore all other quantum numbers of the photon (such as lepton number, baryon number, and flavour quantum numbers) are zero.

Photons are emitted in many natural processes. For example, when a charge is accelerated it emits synchrotron radiation. During a molecular, atomic or nuclear transition to a lower energy level, photons of various energy will be emitted, from infrared light to gamma rays. A photon can also be emitted when a particle and its corresponding antiparticle are annihilated.

In empty space, the photon moves at c (the speed of light) and its energy and momentum are related by $E = pc$, where p is the magnitude of the momentum vector p. For comparison, the corresponding equation for particles with mass m is:

$$E^2 = p^2c^2 + m^2c^4.$$

The energy and momentum of a photon depend only on its frequency (n) or equivalently, its wavelength (λ):

$$E = \hbar\omega = h\nu = \frac{hc}{\lambda}$$

$$\mathbf{p} = \hbar\mathbf{k},$$

where k is the wave vector (with the wave number k = $2\pi/\lambda$ as its magnitude), (!) = $2\pi\nu$ is the angular frequency, and $\hbar$= $h/2\pi$ is the reduced Planck constant.

Since p points in the direction of the photon's propagation, the magnitude of the momentum is

$$p = \hbar k = \frac{h\nu}{c} = \frac{h}{\lambda}.$$

The photon also carries spin angular momentum that does not depend on its frequency. The magnitude of its spin is $\sqrt{2}\hbar$ and the component measured along its direction of motion, its helicity, must be $\pm\hbar$. These two possible helicities, called right-handed and left-handed, correspond to the two possible circular polarization states of the photon.

To illustrate the significance of these formulae, the annihilation of a particle with its antiparticle in free space must result in the creation of at least two photons for the following reason. In the center of mass frame, the colliding antiparticles have no net momentum, whereas a single photon always has momentum (since it is determined, as we have seen, only by the photon's frequency or wavelength — which cannot be zero). Hence, conservation of momentum (or equivalently, translational invariance) requires that at least two photons are created, with zero net momentum. (However it is possible if the system interacts with another particle or field for annihilation to produce one photon, as when a positron annihilates with a bound atomic electron, it is possible for only one photon to be emitted, as the nuclear Coulomb field breaks translational symmetry.) The energy of the two photons-or, equivalently, their frequency-may be determined from conservation of four-momentum. Seen another way, the photon can be considered as its own antiparticle. The reverse process, pair production, is the dominant mechanism by which high-energy photons such as gamma rays lose energy while passing through matter. That process is the reverse of "annihilation to one photon" allowed in the electric field of an atomic nucleus.

The classical formulae for the energy and momentum of electromagnetic radiation can be re-expressed in terms of photon events. For example, the pressure of electromagnetic radiation on an object derives from the transfer of photon momentum per unit time and unit area to that object, since pressure is force per unit area and force is the change in momentum per unit time.

Historical development

In most theories up to the eighteenth century, light was pictured as being made up of particles. One of the earliest particle theories was described in the *Book of Optics* (1021) by Alhazen, who held light rays to be streams of minute particles that "lack all sensible qualities except energy."

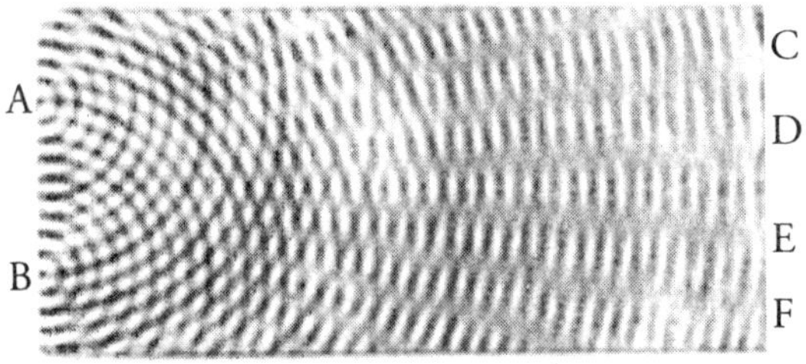

Thomas Young's double-slit experiment in 1805 showed that light can act as a wave, helping to defeat early particle theories of light.

Since particle models cannot easily account for the refraction, diffraction and birefringence of light, wave theories of light were proposed by René Descartes (1637), Robert Hooke (1665), and Christian Huygens (1678); however, particle models remained dominant, chiefly due to the influence of Isaac Newton. In the early nineteenth century, Thomas Young and August Fresnel clearly demonstrated the interference and diffraction of light and by 1850 wave models were generally accepted. In 1865, James Clerk Maxwell's prediction that light was an electromagnetic wave-which was confirmed experimentally in 1888 by

Heinrich Hertz's detection of radio waves-seemed to be the final blow to particle models of light.

The Maxwell wave theory, however, does not account for all properties of light. The Maxwell theory predicts that the energy of a light wave depends only on its intensity, not on its frequency; nevertheless, several independent types of experiments show that the energy imparted by light to atoms depends only on the light's frequency, not on its intensity. For example, some chemical reactions are provoked only by light of frequency higher than a certain threshold; light of frequency lower than the threshold, no matter how intense, does not initiate the reaction. Similarly, electrons can be ejected from a metal plate by shining light of sufficiently high frequency on it (the photoelectric effect); the energy of the ejected electron is related only to the light's frequency, not to its intensity.

Light wave

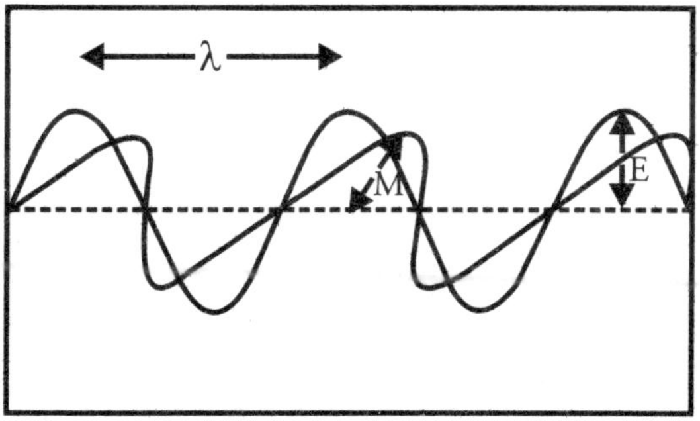

λ = Wave length, E = Amplitude of Electric field,
M = Amplitude of Magnetic field

In 1900, Maxwell's theoretical model of light as oscillating electric and magnetic fields seemed complete. However, several observations could not be explained by any wave model of electromagnetic radiation, leading to the idea that light-energy was packaged into quanta described by $E=hn$. Later experiments showed that these light-quanta also carry momentum and, thus, can be considered particles: the *photon* concept was born, leading to a deeper understanding of the electric and magnetic fields themselves.

At the same time, investigations of blackbody radiation carried out over four decades (1860-1900) by various researchers culminated in Max Planck's hypothesis that the energy of *any* system that absorbs or emits electromagnetic radiation of frequency n is an integer multiple of an energy quantum $E = hn$. As shown by Albert Einstein, some form of energy quantization must be assumed to account for the thermal equilibrium observed between matter and electromagnetic radiation; for this explanation of the photoelectric effect, Einstein received the 1921 Nobel Prize in physics.

Since the Maxwell theory of light allows for all possible energies of electromagnetic radiation, most physicists assumed initially that the energy quantization resulted from some unknown constraint on the matter that absorbs or emits the radiation. In 1905, Einstein was the first to propose that energy quantization was a property of electromagnetic radiation itself. Although he accepted the validity of

Maxwell's theory, Einstein pointed out that many anomalous experiments could be explained if the energy of a Maxwellian light wave were localized into point-like quanta that move independently of one another, even if the wave itself is spread continuously over space. In 1909 and 1916, Einstein showed that, if Planck's law of black-body radiation is accepted, the energy quanta must also carry momentum $p = h / \lambda$, making them full-fledged particles. This photon momentum was observed experimentally by Arthur Compton, for which he received the Nobel Prize in 1927. The pivotal question was then: how to unify Maxwell's wave theory of light with its experimentally observed particle nature? The answer to this question occupied Albert Einstein for the rest of his life, and was solved in quantum electrodynamics and its successor, the Standard Model (see Second quantization and The photon as a gauge boson, below).

In a 1905 paper, Einstein postulated that light itself consists of localized particles (*quanta*). Einstein's light quanta were nearly universally rejected by all physicists, including Max Planck and Niels Bohr. This idea only became universally accepted in 1919, with Robert Millikan's detailed experiments on the photoelectric effect, and with the measurement of Compton scattering.

Einstein's paper on the light particles was almost entirely motivated by thermodynamic considerations. He was not at all motivated by the detailed experiments on the photoelectric effect, which did not confirm his theory until fifteen years later. Einstein considers the entropy of light at temperature T, and decomposes it into a low-frequency part and a high-frequency part. The high-frequency part, where the light is described by Wien's law, has an entropy which looks exactly the same as the entropy of a gas of classical particles.

Since the entropy is the logarithm of the number of possible states, Einstein concludes that the number of states of short wavelength light waves in a box with volume V is equal to the number of states of a group of localizable particles in the same box. Since (unlike others) he was comfortable with the statistical interpretation, he confidently postulates that the light itself is made up of localized particles, as this is the only reasonable interpretation of the entropy.

This leads him to conclude that each wave of frequency f is associated with a collection of photons with energy hf each, where h is Planck's constant. He does not say much more, because he is not sure how the particles are related to the wave. But he does suggest that this idea would explain certain experimental results, notably the photoelectric effect.

Early objections

Einstein's 1905 predictions were verified experimentally in several ways in the first two decades of the 20th century, as recounted in Robert Millikan's Nobel lecture. However, before Compton's experiment showing that photons carried momentum proportional to their wave number (or frequency) (1922), most physicists were reluctant to believe that electromagnetic radiation itself might be particulate. Instead, there was a widespread belief that energy quantization resulted from some unknown constraint on the matter that absorbs or emits radiation. Attitudes changed over gradually. In part, the change can be traced to experiments such as Compton scattering, where it was much more difficult not to ascribe quantization to light itself to explain the observed results.

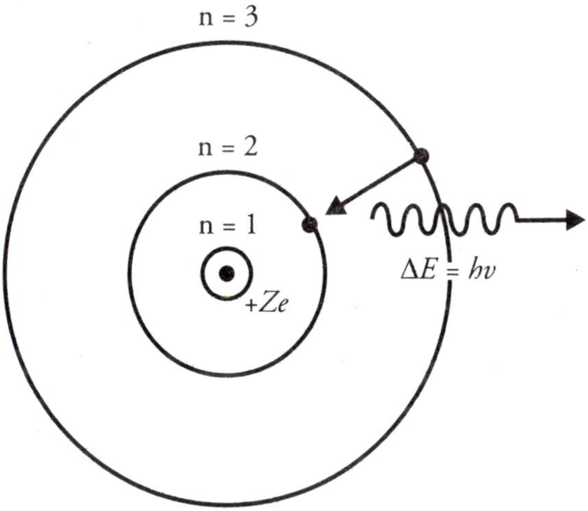

Up to 1923, most physicists were reluctant to accept that light itself was quantized. Instead, they tried to explain photon behaviour by quantizing only matter, as in the Bohr model of the hydrogen atom (shown here). Even though these semiclassical models were only a first approximation, they were accurate for simple systems and they led to quantum mechanics.

Even after Compton's experiment, Bohr, Hendrik Kramers and John Slater made one last attempt to preserve the Maxwellian continuous electromagnetic field model of light, the so-called BKS model. To account for the then-available data, two drastic hypotheses had to be made:

1. Energy and momentum are conserved only on the average in interactions between matter and radiation, not in elementary processes such as absorption and emission. This allows one to reconcile the (at the time believed to be) discontinuously changing energy of the atom (jump between energy states) with the continuous release of energy into radiation. (It is now known that this is actually a continuous process, the combined atom-field system evolving in time according to Schroedinger's equation.)

2. Causality is abandoned. For example, spontaneous emissions are merely emissions induced by a "virtual" electromagnetic field.

However, refined Compton experiments showed that energy-momentum is conserved extraordinarily well in elementary processes; and also that the jolting of the electron and the generation of a new photon in Compton scattering obey causality to within 10 ps. Accordingly, Bohr and his co-workers gave their model "as honorable a funeral as possible". Nevertheless, the failures of the BKS model inspired Werner Heisenberg in his development of matrix mechanics.

A few physicists persisted in developing semiclassical models in which electromagnetic radiation is not quantized, but matter appears to obey the laws of quantum mechanics.

Although the evidence for photons from chemical and physical experiments was overwhelming by the 1970s, this evidence could not be considered as absolutely definitive; since it relied on the interaction of light with matter, a sufficiently complicated theory of matter could in principle account for the evidence. Nevertheless, all semiclassical theories were refuted definitively in the 1970s and 1980s by photon-correlation experiments.

Hence, Einstein's hypothesis that quantization is a property of light itself is considered to be proven.

Quantized Atomic Vibrations

Einstein continued his work on quantum mechanics in 1906, by explaining the specific heat anomaly in solids. This was the first application of quantum theory to a mechanical system. Since Planck's distribution for light oscillators had no problem with infinite specific heats, the same idea could be applied to solids to fix the specific heat problem there. Einstein showed in a simple model that the hypothesis that solid motion is quantized explains why the specific heat of a solid goes to zero at zero temperature.

Einstein's model treats each atom as connected to a single spring. Instead of connecting all the atoms to each other, which leads to standing waves with all sorts of different frequencies, Einstein imagined that each atom was attached to a fixed point in space by a spring. This is not physically correct, but it still predicts that the specific heat is $3Nk_B$, since the number of independent oscillations stays the same.

Einstein then assumes that the motion in this model are quantized, according to the Planck law, so that each independent spring motion has energy which is an integer multiple of hf, where f is the frequency of oscillation. With this assumption, he applied Boltzmann's statistical method to calculate the average energy of the spring. The result was the same as the one that Planck had derived for light: for temperatures where $k_B T$ is much smaller than hf, the motion is frozen, and the specific heat goes to zero.

So Einstein concluded that quantum mechanics would solve the main problem of classical physics, the specific heat anomaly. The particles of sound implied by this formulation are now called phonons. Because all of Einstein's springs have the same stiffness, they all freeze out at the same temperature, and this leads to a prediction that the specific heat should go to zero exponentially fast when the temperature is low. The solution to this problem is to solve for the independent normal modes individually, and to quantize those. Then each normal mode has a different frequency, and long wavelength vibration modes freeze out at colder temperatures than short wavelength ones. This was done by Debye, and after this modification, Einstein's quantization method reproduced quantitatively the behaviour of the specific heats of solids at low temperatures.

This work was the foundation of condensed matter physics.

Einstein solid

The Einstein solid is a model of a solid based on three assumptions:

- Each atom in the lattice is a 3D quantum harmonic oscillator

- Each atom is attached to a preferred position in space by a spring
- All springs have same frequency (contrast with the Debye model)

While the assumption that a solid has independent oscillations is very accurate, these oscillations are sound waves, collective modes involving many atoms. In the Einstein model, each atom oscillates independently. Einstein was aware that the frequency of the actual oscillations would be different, but he nevertheless proposed this theory because it was a particularly clear demonstration that quantum mechanics could solve the specific heat problem in classical mechanics.

Historical impact

The original theory proposed by Einstein in 1907 had a great historical relevance. The heat capacity of solids as predicted by the empirical Dulong-Petit law was required by classical mechanics, the specific heat of solids should be independent of temperature. But experiments at low temperatures showed that the heat capacity changes, going to zero at absolute zero. As the temperature goes up, the specific heat goes up until it approaches the Dulong and Petit prediction at high temperature.

By employing Planck's quantization assumption, Einstein's theory accounted for the observed experimental trend for the first time. Together with the photoelectric effect, this became one of the most important evidence for the need of quantization. Einstein used the levels of the quantum mechanical oscillator many years before the advent of modern quantum mechanics.

In Einstein's model, the specific heat approaches zero exponentially fast at low temperatures. This is because all the oscillations have one common frequency. The correct behaviour is found by quantizing the normal modes of the solid in the same way that Einstein suggested. Then the frequencies of the waves are not all the same, and the specific heat goes to zero as a T3 power law, which matches experiment. This modification is called the Debye Model, which appeared in 1912.

Heat Capacity (Microcanonical Ensemble)

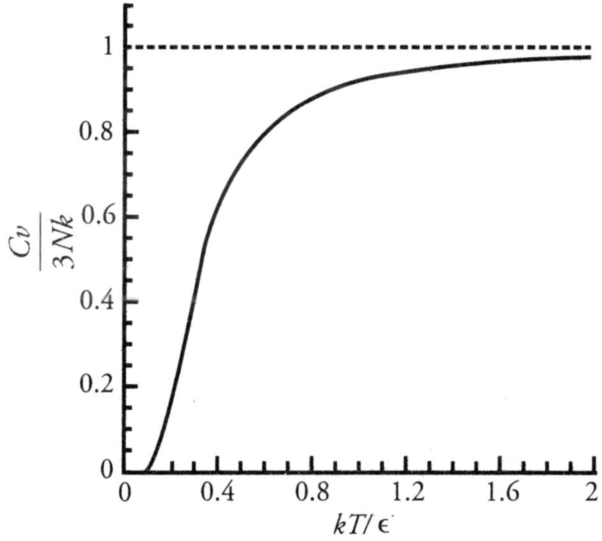

Heat capacity of an *Einstein solid* as a function of temperature. Experimental value of $3Nk$ is recovered at high temperatures.

The heat capacity of an object at constant volume V is defined through the internal energy U as

$$C_V = \left(\frac{\partial U}{\partial T}\right)_V$$

T, the temperature of the system, can be found from the entropy

$$\frac{1}{T} = \frac{\partial S}{\partial U}.$$

To find the entropy consider a solid made of N atoms, each of which has 3 degrees of freedom. So there are 3N quantum harmonic oscillators (hereafter SHOs).

$$N' = 3N$$

Possible energies of an SHO are given by

$$E_n = \hbar\omega\left(n + \frac{1}{2}\right)$$

or, in other words, the energy levels are evenly spaced and one can define a quantum of energy

$$\varepsilon = \hbar\omega$$

which is the smallest and only amount by which the energy of SHO can be incremented. Next, we must compute the multiplicity of the system. That is, compute the number of ways to distribute q quanta of energy among N'SHOs. This task becomes simpler if one thinks of distributing q pebbles over N' boxes

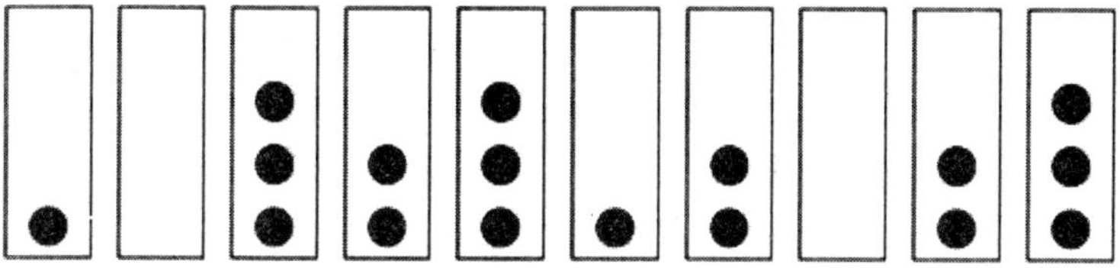

or separating stacks of pebbles with partitions

or arranging q pebbles and N'— 1 partitions

The last picture is the most telling. The number of arrangements of n objects is $n!$. So the number of possible arrangements of q pebbles and N'— 1 partitions is $(q + N'$— 1). However, if partition #2 and partition #5 trade places, no one would notice. The same argument goes for quanta. To obtain the number of possible *distinguishable* arrangements one has to divide the total number of arrangements by the number of *indistinguishable* arrangements. There are $q!$ identical quanta arrangements, and $(N'$— 1) identical partition arrangements. Therefore, multiplicity of the system is given by

$$\Omega = \frac{(q + N' - 1)!}{q!(N' - 1)!}$$

which, as mentioned before, is the number of ways to deposit q quanta of energy into N'—1 oscillators. Entropy of the system has the form

$$S / k = \ln \Omega = \ln \frac{(q + N' - 1)!}{q!(N' - 1)!}.$$

N' is a huge number-subtracting one from it has no overall effect whatsoever:

$$S / k \approx \ln \frac{(q + N')!}{q!N'!}$$

With the help of Stirling's approximation, entropy can be simplified:

$$S / k \approx (q + N') \ln (q + N') - N' \ln N' - q \ln q.$$

Total energy of the solid is given by

$$U = \frac{N'\varepsilon}{2} + q\varepsilon,$$

We are now ready to compute the temperature

$$\frac{1}{T} = \frac{\partial S}{\partial U} = \frac{\partial S}{\partial q}\frac{dq}{dU} = \frac{1}{\varepsilon}\frac{\partial S}{\partial q} = \frac{k}{\varepsilon}\ln(1 + N' / q)$$

Inverting this formula to find U:

$$U = \frac{N'\varepsilon}{2} + \frac{N'\varepsilon}{e^{\varepsilon/kT} - 1}.$$

Differentiating with respect to temperature to find C_V:

$$C_V = \frac{\partial U}{\partial T} = \frac{N'\varepsilon^2}{kT^2} \frac{e^{\varepsilon/kT}}{\left(e^{\varepsilon/kT} - 1\right)^2}$$

or

$$C_V = 3Nk\left(\frac{\varepsilon}{kT}\right)^2 \frac{e^{\varepsilon/kT}}{\left(e^{\varepsilon/kT} - 1\right)^2}.$$

Although Einstein model of the solid predicts the heat capacity accurately at high temperatures, it noticeably deviates from experimental values at low temperatures.

Heat Capacity (Canonical Ensemble)

Heat capacity can be obtained through the use of the canonical partition function of an SHO.

$$Z = \sum_{n=0}^{\infty} e^{-E_n/kT}$$

where

$$E_n = \varepsilon \quad E_n = \varepsilon\left(n + \frac{1}{2}\right)$$

substituting this into the partition function formula yields

$$Z = \sum_{n=0}^{\infty} e^{-\varepsilon(n+1/2)/kT} = e^{-\varepsilon/2kT} \sum_{n=0}^{\infty} e^{-n\varepsilon/kT} = e^{-\varepsilon/2kT} \sum_{n=0}^{\infty} \left(e^{-\varepsilon/kT}\right)^n$$

$$= \frac{e^{-\varepsilon/2kT}}{1-e^{-\varepsilon/kT}} = \frac{1}{e^{\varepsilon/2kT} - e^{-\varepsilon/2kT}} = \frac{1}{2\sinh\left(\dfrac{\varepsilon}{2kT}\right)}.$$

This is the partition function of one SHO. Because, statistically, heat capacity, energy, and entropy of the solid are equally distributed among its atoms (SHOs), we can work with this partition function to obtain those quantities and then simply multiply them by N' to get the total. Next, let's compute the average energy of each oscillator

$$\langle E \rangle = u = -\frac{1}{Z}\partial_\beta Z$$

where

$$\beta = \frac{1}{kT}.$$

Therefore

$$u = -2\sinh\left(\frac{\varepsilon}{2kT}\right) \frac{-\cosh\left(\dfrac{\varepsilon}{2kT}\right)}{2\sinh^2\left(\dfrac{\varepsilon}{2kT}\right)} \frac{\varepsilon}{2} = \frac{\varepsilon}{2}\coth\left(\frac{\varepsilon}{2kT}\right).$$

Heat capacity of one oscillator is then

$$C_V = \frac{\partial u}{\partial T} = -\frac{\varepsilon}{2} \frac{1}{\sinh^2\left(\dfrac{\varepsilon}{2kT}\right)} \left(-\frac{\varepsilon}{2kT^2}\right)$$

$$= k\left(\frac{\varepsilon}{2kT}\right)^2 \frac{1}{\sinh^2\left(\frac{\varepsilon}{2kT}\right)}.$$

Up to now, we calculated the heat capacity of a unique degree of freedom, which has been modeled as an SHO. The heat capacity of the entire solid is then given by $Cn = 3NC_n$, where the total number of degree of freedom of the solid is three (for the three directional degree of freedom) times N, the number of atoms in the solid. One thus obtains

$$C_V = 3Nk\left(\frac{\varepsilon}{2kT}\right)^2 \frac{1}{\sinh^2\left(\frac{\varepsilon}{2kT}\right)}.$$

which is algebraically identical to the formula derived in the previous section.

The quantity $T_E = \varepsilon / k$ has the dimensions of temperature and is a characteristic property of a crystal. It is known as "Einstein's Temperature". Hence, the Einstein Crystal model predicts that the energy and heat capacities of a crystal are universal functions of the dimensionless ratio $T\ /\ T_E$. Similarly, the Debye model predicts a universal function of the ratio T/T_D.

Adiabatic Principle and Action-Angle Variables

Throughout the 1910s, quantum mechanics expanded in scope to cover many different systems. After Ernest Rutherford discovered the nucleus and proposed that electrons orbit like planets, Niels Bohr was able to show that the same quantum mechanical postulates introduced by Planck and developed by Einstein would explain the discrete motion of electrons in atoms, and the periodic table of the elements.

Einstein contributed to these developments by linking them with the 1898 arguments Wilhelm Wien had made. Wien had shown that the hypothesis of adiabatic invariance of a thermal equilibrium state allows all the blackbody curves at different temperature to be derived from one another by a simple shifting process. Einstein noted in 1911 that the same adiabatic principle shows that the quantity which is quantized in any mechanical motion must be an adiabatic invariant. Arnold Sommerfeld identified this adiabatic invariant as the action variable of classical mechanics. The law that the action variable is quantized was the basic principle of the quantum theory as it was known between 1900 and 1925.

Old Quantum Theory

The old quantum theory was a collection of results from the years 1900-1925 which predate modern quantum mechanics. The theory was never complete or self-consistent, but was a collection of heuristic prescriptions which are now understood to be the first quantum corrections to classical mechanics. The Bohr model was the focus of study, and Arnold Sommerfeld made a crucial contribution by quantizing the Z-component of the angular momentum, which in the old quantum era was inappropriately called *space quantization* (Richtungsquantelung).

The main tool was Bohr Sommerfeld quantization, a procedure for selecting out certain discrete set of states of a classical integrable motion as allowed states. These are like the allowed orbits of the Bohr model of the atom, the system can only be in one of these states, and not in any states in between. The theory did not extend to chaotic motions, because it required a full multiply periodic trajectory of the classical system for all time in order to pose the quantum conditions.

The old quantum theory lives on as an approximation technique in quantum mechanics, called the WKB method. Semi-classical approximations were a popular research subject in the 1970s and 1980s, after Gutzwiller discovered a semi-classical description for systems which are classically chaotic.

Basic principles

The basic idea of the old quantum theory is that the motion in an atomic system is quantized, or discrete. The system obeys classical mechanics except that not every motion is allowed, only those motions which obey the *old quantum condition*:

$$\oint_{H(p,q)=E} p_i dq_i = n_i h$$

where the *pi* are the momenta of the system and the *qi* are the corresponding coordinates. The quantum numbers *ni* are *integers* and the integral is taken over one period of the motion. The integral is an area in phase space, which is a quantity called the action, which is quantized in units of Planck's constant. For this reason, Planck's constant was often called the *quantum of action.*

In order for the old quantum condition to make sense, the classical motion must be separable, meaning that there are separate coordinates *qi* in terms of which the motion is periodic. The periods of the different motions do not have to be the same, they can even be incommensurate, but there must be a set of coordinates where the motion decomposes in a multi-periodic way.

The motivation for the old quantum condition was the correspondence principle, complemented by the physical observation that the quantities which are quantized must be adiabatic invariants. Given Planck's quantization rule for the harmonic oscillator, either condition determines the correct classical quantity to quantize in a general system up to an additive constant.

De Broglie waves

In 1905, Einstein noted that the entropy of the quantized electromagnetic field oscillators in a box is, for short wavelength, equal to the entropy of a gas of point particles in the same box. The number of point particles is equal to the number of quanta. Einstein concluded that the quanta were localizable objects, particles of light, and named them photons.

Einstein's theoretical argument was based on thermodynamics, on counting the number of states, and so was not completely convincing. Nevertheless, he concluded that light had attributes of both waves and particles, more precisely that an electromagnetic standing wave with frequency ω with the quantized energy:

$$E = n\hbar\omega$$

should be thought of as consisting of N photons each with an energy. Einstein could not describe how the photons were related to the wave.

The photons have momentum as well as energy, and the momentum had to be where k is the wavenumber of the electromagnetic wave. This is required by relativity, because the momentum and energy form a four-vector, as do the frequency and wave-number.

In 1924, as a PhD candidate, Louis de Broglie proposed a new interpretation of the quantum condition. He suggested that all matter, electrons as well as photons, are described by waves obeying the relations.

$$p = \hbar k$$

or, expressed in terms of wavelength λ instead,

$$p = \frac{h}{\lambda}$$

He then noted that the quantum condition:

$$\int p dx = \hbar \int k dx = 2\pi \hbar n$$

counts the change in phase for the wave as it travels along the classical orbit, and requires that it be an integer multiple of 2π. Expressed in wavelengths, the number of wavelengths along a classical orbit must be an integer. This is the condition for constructive interference, and it explained the reason for quantized orbits-the matter waves make standing waves only at discrete frequencies, at discrete energies.

For example, for a particle confined in a box, a standing wave must fit an integer number of wavelengths twice the distance between the walls. The condition becomes:

$$n\lambda = 2L$$

so that the quantized momenta are:

$$p = \frac{nh}{2L}$$

reproducing the old quantum energy levels.

This development was given a more mathematical form by Einstein, who noted that the phase function for the waves: q(J,x) in a mechanical system should be identified with the solution to the Hamilton-Jacobi equation, an equation which even Hamilton considered to be a short-wavelength limit of a wave mechanics.

These ideas led to the development of Schrödinger equation.

History

The old quantum theory was sparked by the work of Max Planck on the emission and absorption of light, and began in earnest after the work of Albert Einstein on the specific heats of solids. Einstein, followed by Debye, applied quantum principles to the motion of atoms, explaining the specific heat anomaly.

In 1913, Niels Bohr identified the correspondence principle and used it to formulate a model of the Hydrogen atom which explained the line spectrum. In the next few years Arnold Sommerfeld extended the quantum rule to arbitrary integrable systems making use of the principle of adiabatic invariance of the quantum numbers introduced by Lorentz and Einstein. Sommerfeld's model was much closer to the modern quantum mechanical picture than Bohr's.

Throughout the 1910s and well into the 1920s, many problems were attacked using the old quantum theory with mixed results. Molecular rotation and vibration spectra were understood and the electron's spin was discovered, leading to the confusion of half-integer quantum numbers. Max Planck introduced the zero point energy and Arnold Sommerfeld semiclassically quantized the relativistic hydrogen atom. Hendrik Kramers explained the stark effect. Bose and Einstein gave the correct quantum statistics for photons.

Kramers gave a prescription for calculating transition probabilities between quantum states in terms of Fourier components of the motion, ideas which were extended in collaboration with Werner Heisenberg to a semiclassical matriX-like description of atomic transition probabilities. Heisenberg went on to reformulate all of quantum theory in terms of a version of these transition matrices, creating Matrix mechanics.

In 1924, Louis de Broglie introduced the wave theory of matter, which was extended to a semiclassical equation for matter waves by Albert Einstein a short time later. In 1926 Erwin Schrödinger found a completely quantum mechanical wave-equation, which reproduced all the successes of the old quantum theory without ambiguities and inconsistencies. Schrödinger's wave mechanics developed separately from matrix mechanics until Schrödinger and others proved that the two methods predicted the same experimental consequences. Paul Dirac later proved in 1926 that both methods can be obtained from a more general method called transformation theory.

Matrix mechanics and wave mechanics put an end to the era of the old-quantum theory.

Wave-Particle Duality

Although the patent office promoted Einstein to Technical Examiner Second Class in 1906, he had not given up on academia. In 1908, he became a *privatdozent* at the University of Bern. In "über die Entwicklung unserer Anschauungen über das Wesen und die Konstitution der Strahlung" ("The Development of Our Views on the Composition and Essence of Radiation"), on the quantization of light, and in an earlier 1909 paper, Einstein showed that Max Planck's energy quanta must have well-defined momenta and act in some respects as independent, point-like particles. This paper introduced the *photon* concept (although the name *photon* was introduced later by Gilbert N. Lewis in 1926) and inspired the notion of wave-particle duality in quantum mechanics.

In physics and chemistry, wave-particle duality is the concept that all energy (and thus all matter) exhibits both wave-like and particle-like properties. Being a central concept of quantum mechanics, this duality addresses the inadequacy of classical concepts like "particle" and "wave" in fully describing the behaviour of quantum-scale objects. Orthodox interpretations of quantum mechanics explain this ostensible paradox as a fundamental property of the Universe, while alternative interpretations explain the duality as an emergent, second-order consequence of various limitations of the observer. This treatment focuses on explaining the behaviour from the perspective of the widely used Copenhagen interpretation.

Wave-particle duality should be distinguished from wave-particle complementarity, the latter being an extension of the duality. Complementarity states that, within the base concept that all classical waves are composed of quanta/particles exhibiting the overall wave pattern and all particles behave as waves according to the de Broglie wavelength, these "wavicles" exhibit a freedom to behave in more "wave-like" or more "particle-like" manners (these behaviours being mutually exclusive).

The idea of duality originated in a debate over the nature of light and matter dating back to the 1600s, when competing theories of light were proposed by Christiaan Huygens and Isaac Newton: light was thought either to consist of waves (Huygens) or of corpuscles/particles (Newton). Through the work of Max Planck, Albert Einstein, Louis de Broglie, Arthur Compton, and many others, current scientific theory holds that all particles also have a wave nature (and vice versa). This phenomenon has been verified not only for elementary particles, but also for compound particles like atoms and even molecules. In fact, according to traditional formulations of non-relativistic quantum mechanics, wave-particle duality applies to all objects, even macroscopic ones; but because of their small wavelengths, the wave properties of macroscopic objects cannot be detected.

Einstein's explanation of The Photoelectric Effect

The photoelectric effect is a phenomenon in which electrons are emitted from matter (metals and non-metallic solids, liquids or gases) as a consequence of their absorption of energy from electromagnetic radiation of very short wavelength, such as visible or ultraviolet light. Electrons emitted in this manner may be referred to as "photoelectrons". As it was first observed by Heinrich Hertz in 1887, the phenomenon is also known as the "Hertz effect", although the latter term has fallen out of general use. Hertz observed and then showed that electrodes illuminated with ultraviolet light create electric sparks more easily.

The photoelectric effect takes place with photons with energies from about a few electronvolts to, in high atomic number elements, over 1 MeV. At the high photon energies comparable to the electron rest energy of 511 keV, Compton scattering, another process, may take place, and above twice this (1.022 MeV) pair production may take place.

Study of the photoelectric effect led to important steps in understanding the quantum nature of light and electrons and influenced the formation of the concept of wave-particle duality.

The term may also, but incorrectly, refer to related phenomena such as the photoconductive effect (also known as photoconductivity or photoresistivity), the photovoltaic effect, or the photoelectrochemical effect which are, in fact, distinctly different.

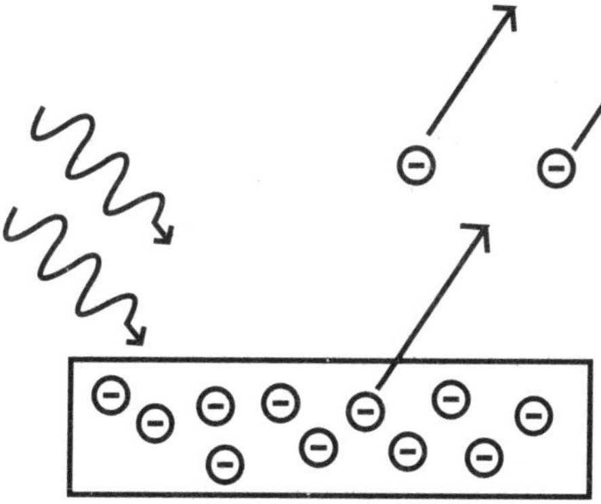

The photoelectric effect. Incoming photons on the left strike a metal plate (bottom), and eject electrons, depicted as flying off to the right.

In 1905, Albert Einstein provided an explanation of the photoelectric effect, a hitherto troubling experiment that the wave theory of light seemed incapable of explaining. He did so by postulating the existence of photons, quanta of light energy with particulate qualities.

In the photoelectric effect, it was observed that shining a light on certain metals would lead to an electric current in a circuit. Presumably, the light was knocking electrons out of the metal, causing current to flow. However, it was also observed that while a dim blue light was enough to cause a current, even the strongest, brightest red light caused no current at all. According to wave theory, the strength or amplitude of a light wave was in proportion to its brightness: a bright light should have been easily strong enough to create a large current. Yet, oddly, this was not so.

Einstein explained this conundrum by postulating that the electrons can receive energy from electromagnetic field only in discrete portions (quanta that were called photons): an amount of energy E that was related to the frequency f of the light by

$$E = hf$$

...where h is Planck's constant (6.626×10^{-34} J seconds). Only photons of a high enough frequency (above a certain *threshold* value) could knock an electron free. For example, photons of blue light had sufficient energy to free an electron from the metal, but photons of red light did not. More intense light above the threshold frequency could release more electrons, but no amount of light below the threshold frequency could release an electron.

Einstein was awarded the Nobel Prize in Physics in 1921 for his theory of the photoelectric effect.

Theory of Critical Opalescence

Critical opalescence is a phenomenon which arises in the region of a continuous, or second-order, phase transition. Originally reported by Thomas Andrews in 1869 for the liquid-gas transition in carbon dioxide, many other examples have been discovered since. The phenomenon is most commonly demonstrated in binary fluid mixtures, such as methanol and cyclohexane. As the critical point is approached the sizes of the gas and liquid region begin to fluctuate over increasingly large length scales. As the density fluctuations become of a size comparable to the wavelength of light, the light is scattered and causes the normally transparent fluid to appear cloudy. Tellingly, the opalescence does not diminish as one gets closer to the critical point, where the largest fluctuations can reach even centimetre proportions, confirming the physical relevance of smaller fluctuations.

In 1908 the Polish physicist Marian Smoluchowski became the first to ascribe the phenomenon of critical opalescence to large density fluctuations. In 1920 Albert

Einstein showed that the link between critical opalescence and Rayleigh scattering is quantitative.

Einstein returned to the problem of thermodynamic fluctuations, giving a treatment of the density variations in a fluid at its critical point. Ordinarily the density fluctuations are controlled by the second derivative of the free energy with respect to the density. At the critical point, this derivative is zero, leading to large fluctuations. The effect of density fluctuations is that light of all wavelengths is scattered, making the fluid look milky white. Einstein relates this to Raleigh scattering, which is what happens when the fluctuation size is much smaller than the wavelength, and which explains why the sky is blue.

Zero-Point Energy

In physics, the zero-point energy is the lowest possible energy that a quantum mechanical physical system may have and is the energy of the ground state. The quantum mechanical system that encapsulates this energy is the zero-point field. The concept was first proposed by Albert Einstein and Otto Stern in 1913. The term "zero-point energy" is a calque of the German Nullpunktenergie. All quantum mechanical systems have a zero-point energy. The term arises commonly in reference to the ground state of the quantum harmonic oscillator and its null oscillations.

Zero-point energy is sometimes used as a synonym for the vacuum energy, an amount of energy associated with the vacuum of empty space. When the term is used in this way, sometimes it is referred to as the quantum vacuum zero point energy. In cosmology, the vacuum energy is one possible explanation for the cosmological constant. The variation in zero-point energy as the boundaries of a region of vacuum move leads to the Casimir effect, which is observable in nanoscale devices.

A related term is zero-point field, which is the lowest energy state of a field; i.e. its ground state, which is non-Zero.

History

In the year 1900, Max Planck derived the formula for the energy of a single "energy radiator", i.e. a vibrating atomic unit, as:

$$\epsilon = \frac{h\nu}{e^{\frac{h\nu}{kT}} - 1}$$

where *h* is Planck's constant, *n* is the frequency, *k* is Boltzmann's constant, and *T* is the absolute temperature.

Then in 1913, using this formula as a basis, Albert Einstein and Otto Stern published a paper of great significance in which they suggested for the first time the existence of a residual energy that all oscillators have at absolute zero. They called this "residual energy" and then Nullpunktsenergie (in German), which later became translated as *zero-point energy*. They carried out an analysis of the specific heat of hydrogen gas at low temperature, and concluded that the data are best represented if the vibrational energy is taken to have the form:

$$\epsilon = \frac{h\nu}{e^{\frac{h\nu}{kT}} - 1} + \frac{h\nu}{2}$$

According to this expression, an atomic system at absolute zero retains an energy of ½hν.

Foundational physics

The energy of a system is relative, and is defined only in relation to some given state (often called the reference state). One might associate a motionless system with zero energy, but doing so is purely arbitrary. In quantum physics, it is natural to associate the energy with the expectation value of a certain operator, the Hamiltonian of the system. For almost all quantum-mechanical systems, the lowest possible expectation value of this operator, which would be the zero-point energy, is not zero. Adding an arbitrary constant to the Hamiltonian gives an equivalent description of the physical system, but can make the zero-point energy different. Regardless of what constant is added to the Hamiltonian, the minimum momentum is always the same non-Zero value.

Varieties

The concept of zero-point energy occurs in a number of situations.

In ordinary quantum mechanics, the zero-point energy is the energy associated with the ground state of the system. The most famous such example is the energy $E = \hbar\omega/2$ associated with the ground state of the quantum harmonic oscillator. More precisely, the zero-point energy is the expectation value of the Hamiltonian of the system.

In quantum field theory, the fabric of space is visualized as consisting of fields, with the field at every point in space and time being a quantized simple harmonic oscillator, with neighboring oscillators interacting. In this case, one has a contribution of $E=\hbar\omega/2$ from every point in space, resulting in a calculation of infinite zero-point energy. The zero-point energy is again the expectation value of the Hamiltonian; here, however, the phrase vacuum expectation value is more commonly used, and the energy is called the vacuum energy.

In quantum perturbation theory, it is sometimes said that the contribution of one-loop and multi-loop Feynman diagrams to elementary particle propagators are the contribution of vacuum fluctuations or the zero-point energy to the particle masses.

Experimental observations

A phenomenon that is commonly presented as evidence for the existence of zero-point energy in vacuum is the Casimir effect, proposed in 1948 by Dutch physicist Hendrik B. G. Casimir (Philips Research), who considered the quantized electromagnetic field between a pair of grounded, neutral metal plates. The vacuum energy contains contributions from all wavelengths, except those excluded by the spacing between plates. As the plates draw together, more wavelengths are excluded and the vacuum energy decreases. The decrease in energy means there must be a force doing work on the plates as they move. This force has been measured and found to be in good agreement with the theory. However, there is still some debate on whether vacuum energy explains the Casimir effect as the force can be explained equally well by a different theory involving charge-current interactions (the radiation-reaction picture), as argued by Robert Jaffe of MIT.

The experimentally measured Lamb shift has been argued to be, in part, a zero-point energy effect.

Gravitation and cosmology

In cosmology, the zero-point energy offers an intriguing possibility for explaining the speculative positive values of the proposed cosmological constant. In brief, if the energy is "really there", then it should exert a gravitational force. In general relativity, mass and energy are equivalent; both produce a gravitational field. One obvious difficulty with this association is that the zero-point energy of the vacuum is absurdly large. Naively, it is infinite, but only differences in energy are physically measurable. The infinity can be removed by renormalization. In all practical calculations, this is how the infinity is handled. It is also arguable that new physics takes over at the Planck scale, and that the energy growth is cut off at that point.

Principle of Equivalence

In the physics of general relativity, the equivalence principle refers to several related concepts dealing with the equivalence of gravitational and inertial mass, and to Albert Einstein's assertion that the gravitational "force" as experienced locally while standing on a massive body (such as the Earth) is actually the same as the pseudo-force experienced by an observer in a non-inertial (accelerated) frame of reference.

Einstein's statement of the equivalence principle

A little reflection will show that the law of the equality of the inertial and gravitational mass is equivalent to the assertion that the acceleration imparted to a body by a gravitational field is independent of the nature of the body. For Newton's equation of motion in a gravitational field, written out in full, it is: (Inertial mass) (Acceleration) = (Intensity of the gravitational field) (Gravitational mass). It is only when there is numerical equality between the inertial and gravitational mass that the acceleration is independent of the nature of the body.

Development of gravitation theory

Something like the equivalence principle emerged in the late 16th and early 17th centuries, when Galileo expressed experimentally that the acceleration of a test mass due to gravitation is independent of the amount of mass being accelerated. These findings led to gravitational theory, in which the inertial and gravitational masses are identical.

The equivalence principle proper was introduced by Albert Einstein in 1907, when he observed that the acceleration of bodies towards the center of the Earth at a rate of 1*g* ($g = 9.81$ m/s^2 being a standard reference of gravitational acceleration at the Earth's surface) is equivalent to the acceleration of an inertially moving body that would be observed on a rocket in free space being accelerated at a rate of 1g. Einstein stated it thus:

"we assume the complete physical equivalence of a gravitational field and a corresponding acceleration of the reference system." (Einstein 1907).

That is, being at rest on the surface of the Earth is equivalent to being inside a spaceship (far from any sources of gravity) that is being accelerated by its engines. From this principle, Einstein deduced that free-fall is actually inertial motion. By contrast, in Newtonian mechanics, gravity is assumed to be a force. This force draws objects having mass towards the center of any massive body. At the Earth's surface, the force of gravity is counteracted by the mechanical (physical) resistance of the Earth's surface. So in Newtonian physics, a person at rest on the surface of a (non-rotating) massive object is in an inertial frame of reference. These considerations suggest the following corollary to the equivalence principle, which Einstein formulated precisely in 1911:

"Whenever an observer detects the local presence of a force that acts on all objects in direct proportion to the inertial mass of each object, that observer is in an accelerated frame of reference."

Einstein also referred to two reference frames, *K* and *K'*. *K* is a uniform gravitational field, whereas *K'* has no gravitational field but is uniformly accelerated such that objects in the two frames experience identical forces:

"We arrive at a very satisfactory interpretation of this law of experience, if we assume that the systems K and K' are physically exactly equivalent, that is, if we assume that we may just as well regard the system K as being in a space free from gravitational fields, if we then regard K as uniformly accelerated. This assumption of exact physical equivalence makes it impossible for us to speak of the absolute acceleration of the system of reference, just as the usual theory of relativity forbids us to talk of the absolute velocity of a system; and it makes the equal falling of all bodies in a gravitational field seem a matter of course." (Einstein 1911)

This observation was the start of a process that culminated in general relativity. Einstein suggested that it should be elevated to the status of a general principle when constructing his theory of relativity:

"As long as we restrict ourselves to purely mechanical processes in the realm where Newton's mechanics holds sway, we are certain of the equivalence of the systems K and K'. But this view of ours will not have any deeper significance unless the systems K and K' are equivalent with respect to all physical processes, that is, unless the laws of nature with respect to K are in entire agreement with those with respect to K'. By assuming this to be so, we arrive at a principle which, if it is really true, has great heuristic importance. For by theoretical consideration of processes which take place relatively to a system of reference with uniform acceleration, we obtain information as to the career of processes in a homogeneous gravitational field." (Einstein 1911)

Einstein combined the equivalence principle with special relativity to predict that clocks run at different rates in a gravitational potential, and light rays bend in a gravitational field, even before he developed the concept of curved spacetime.

So the original equivalence principle, as described by Einstein, concluded that free-fall and inertial motion were physically equivalent. This form of the equivalence principle can be stated as follows. An observer in a windowless room cannot distinguish between being on the surface of the Earth, and being in a spaceship in deep space accelerating at 1g. This is not strictly true, because massive bodies give rise to tidal effects (caused by variations in the strength and direction of the gravitational field) which are absent from an accelerating spaceship in deep space.

Although the equivalence principle guided the development of general relativity, it is not a founding principle of relativity but rather a simple consequence of the *geometrical* nature of the theory. In general relativity, objects in free-fall follow geodesics of spacetime, and what we perceive as the force of gravity is instead a result of our being unable to follow those geodesics of spacetime, because the mechanical resistance of matter prevents us from doing so.

Since Einstein developed general relativity, there was a need to develop a framework to test the theory against other possible theories of gravity compatible with special relativity. This was developed by Robert Dicke as part of his program to test general relativity. Two new principles were suggested, the so-called Einstein equivalence principle and the strong equivalence principle, each of which assumes the weak equivalence principle as a starting point. They only differ in whether or not they apply to gravitational experiments.

Modern usage

Three forms of the equivalence principle are in current use: weak, Einsteinian, and strong.

The weak equivalence principle

The discovery of weak equivalence principle

Loránd Eötvös published on surface tension between 1876 and 1886. The Torsion or Eötvös balance, designed by Hungarian Baron Loránd Eötvös, is a sensitive instrument for measuring the density of underlying rock strata. The device measures not only the direction of force of gravity, but the change in the force of gravity's extent in horizontal plane. It determines the distribution of masses in the Earth's crust. The Eötvös torsion balance, an important instrument of geodesy and geophysics throughout the whole world, studies the Earth's physical properties. It is used for mine exploration, and also in the search for minerals, such as oil, coal and ores. Eötvös' law of capillarity (weak equivalence principle) served as a basis for Einstein's theory of relativity. (Capillarity: the property or exertion of capillary attraction or repulsion, a force that is the resultant of adhesion, cohesion, and surface tension in liquids which are in contact with solids, causing the liquid surface to rise — or be depressed...) These experiments demonstrate that all objects fall at the same rate with negligible friction (including air resistance). The simplest way to test the weak equivalence principle is to drop two objects of different masses or compositions in a vacuum, and see if they hit the ground at the same time. More sophisticated tests use a torsion balance of a type invented by Loránd Eötvös. Satellite experiments are planned for more accurate experiments in space. They verify the weak principle.

The weak equivalence principle, also known as the universality of free fall:

The trajectory of a falling test particle depends only on its initial position and velocity, and is independent of its composition.

or

All test particles at the alike spacetime point in a given gravitational field will undergo the same acceleration, independent of their properties, including their rest mass.

The principle does not apply to large bodies, which might experience tidal forces, or heavy bodies, whose presence will substantially change the gravitational field around them. This form of the equivalence principle is closest to Einstein's original statement: in fact, his statements imply this one.

Active, Passive, and Inertial Masses

By definition of active and passive gravitational mass, the force on M1 due to the gravitational field of M_0 is:

$$F_1 = \frac{M_0^{\text{act}} M_1^{\text{pass}}}{r^2}$$

Likewise the force on a second object of arbitrary mass2 due to the gravitational field of mass 0 is:

$$F_2 = \frac{M_0^{\text{act}} M_2^{\text{pass}}}{r^2}$$

By definition of inertial mass:

$$F = m^{\text{inert}} a$$

If m_1 and m_2 are the same distance r from m0 then, by the weak equivalence principle, they fall at the same rate (i.e. their accelerations are the same)

$$a_1 = \frac{F_1}{m_1^{\text{inert}}} = a_2 = \frac{F_2}{m_2^{\text{inert}}}$$

Hence:

$$\frac{M_0^{\text{act}} M_1^{\text{pass}}}{r^2 m_1^{\text{inert}}} = \frac{M_0^{\text{act}} M_2^{\text{pass}}}{r^2 m_2^{\text{inert}}}$$

Therefore:

$$\frac{M_1^{\text{pass}}}{m_1^{\text{inert}}} = \frac{M_2^{\text{pass}}}{m_2^{\text{inert}}}$$

In other words, passive gravitational mass must be proportional to inertial mass for all objects.

Furthermore by Newton's third law of motion:

$$F_1 = \frac{M_0^{\text{act}} M_1^{\text{pass}}}{r^2}$$

must be equal and opposite to

$$F_0 = \frac{M_1^{\text{act}} M_0^{\text{pass}}}{r^2}$$

It follows that:

$$\frac{M_0^{\text{act}}}{M_0^{\text{pass}}} = \frac{M_1^{\text{act}}}{M_1^{\text{pass}}}$$

In other words, passive gravitational mass must be proportional to active gravitational mass for all objects.

The Einstein equivalence principle

The Einstein equivalence principle states that the weak equivalence principle holds, and that:

The outcome of any local non-gravitational experiment in a freely falling laboratory is independent of the velocity of the laboratory and its location in spacetime.

Here "local" has a very special meaning: not only must the experiment look outside the laboratory, but it must also be small compared to variations in the gravitational field, tidal forces, so that the entire laboratory is freely falling. It also implies the absence of interactions with "external" fields *other than the gravitational field.*

The principle of relativity implies that the outcome of local experiments must be independent of the velocity of the apparatus, so the most important consequence of this principle is the Copernican idea that dimensionless physical values such as the fine-structure constant and electron-to-proton mass ratio must not depend on where in space or time we measure them. Many physicists believe that any Lorentz invariant theory that satisfies the weak equivalence principle also satisfies the Einstein equivalence principle.

Schiff's conjecture suggests that the weak equivalence principle actually implies the Einstein equivalence principle, but it has not been proven. Nonetheless, the two principles are tested with very different kinds of experiments. The Einstein equivalence principle has been criticized as imprecise, because there is no universally accepted way to distinguish gravitational from non-gravitational experiments.

Hole Argument

In general relativity, the hole argument is a "paradox" which much troubled Albert Einstein while developing his famous field equation.

It is interpreted by some philosophers as an argument *against manifold substantialism,* a doctrine that the manifold of events in spacetime are a "substance" which exists independently of the matter within it. Physicists disagree with this interpretation, and view the argument as a confusion about gauge invariance and gauge fixing instead.

Einstein's hole argument

In a usual field equation, knowing the source of the field determines the field everywhere. For example, if we are given the current and charge density and appropriate boundary conditions, Maxwell's equations determine the electric and magnetic fields. They do not determine the vector potential though, because the vector potential depends on an arbitrary choice of gauge.

Einstein noticed that if the equations of gravity are generally covariant, then the metric cannot be determined uniquely by its sources as a function of the coordinates of spacetime. The argument is obvious: consider a gravitational source, such as the sun. Then there is some gravitational field described by a metric $g(r)$. Now perform a coordinate transformation r $r'$where r' is the same as r for points which are inside the sun but r' is different from r outside the sun. The coordinate description of the interior of the sun is unaffected by the transformation, but the functional form of the metric for coordinate values outside the sun is changed.

This means that one source, the sun, can be the source of many seemingly different metrics. The resolution is immediate: any two fields which only differ by a coordinate transformation are physically equivalent, just as two different vector potentials which differ by a gauge transformation are equivalent. Then all these different fields are not different at all.

There are many variations on this apparent paradox. In one version, you consider an initial value surface with some data and find the metric as a function of time. Then you perform a coordinate transformation which moves points around in the future of the initial value surface, but which doesn't affect the initial surface or any points at infinity. Then you can conclude that the generally covariant field equations don't determine the future uniquely, since this new coordinate transformed metric is an equally valid solution. So the initial value problem is unsolvable in general relativity. This is also true in electrodynamics — since you can do a gauge transformation which will only affect the vector potential tomorrow. The resolution in both cases is to use extra conditions to fix a gauge.

Meaning of coordinate invariance

For the philosophically inclined, there is still some subtlety. If the metric components are considered the dynamical variables of General Relativity, the condition that the equations are coordinate invariant doesn't have any content by itself. All physical theories are invariant under coordinate transformations if formulated properly. It is possible to write down Maxwell's equations in any coordinate system, and predict the future in the same way.

But in order to formulate electromagnetism in an arbitrary coordinate system, one must introduce a description of the space-time geometry which is not tied down to a special coordinate system. This description is a metric tensor at every point, or a connection which defines which nearby vectors are parallel. The mathematical object introduced, the Minkowski metric, changes form from one coordinate system to another, but it isn't part of the dynamics, it doesn't obey equations of motion. No matter what happens to the electromagnetic field, it is always the same. It acts without being acted upon.

In General Relativity, every separate local quantity which is used to describe the geometry is itself a local dynamical field, with its own equation of motion. This produces severe restrictions, because the equation of motion has to be a sensible one. It must determine the future from initial conditions, it must not have runaway instabilities for small perturbations, it must define a positive definite energy for small deviations. If one takes the point of view that coordinate invariance is trivially true, the principle of coordinate invariance simply states that the metric itself is dynamical and its equation of motion does not involve a fixed background geometry.

Einstein's resolution

In 1915, Einstein realized that the hole argument makes an assumption about the nature of spacetime, it presumes that the gravitational field as a function of the coordinate labels is physically meaningful by itself. By dropping this assumption general covariance became compatible with determinism, but now the gravitational field is only physically meaningful to the extent that it alters the trajectories of material particles. While two fields that differ by a coordinate transformation look different mathematically, after the trajectories of all the particles are relabeled in the new coordinates, their interactions are manifestly unchanged. This was the first clear statement of the principle of gauge invariance in physical law.

Einstein believed that the hole argument implies that the only meaningful definition of location and time is through matter. A point in spacetime is meaningless in itself, because the label which one gives to such a point is undetermined.

Spacetime points only acquire their physical significance because matter is moving through them. In his words:

"All our spacetime verifications invariably amount to a determination of spacetime coincidences. If, for example, events consisted merely in the motion of material points, then ultimately nothing would be observable but the meeting of two or more of these points." *(Einstein, 1916, p.117)*

He considered this the deepest insight of general relativity. When asked by reporters to summarize his theory, he said:

"People before me believed that if all the matter in the universe were removed, only space and time would exist. My theory proves that space and time would disappear along with matter."

General Relativity

Creation of General Relativity

Early investigations

As Albert Einstein later said, the reason for the development of general relativity was that the preference of inertial motions within special relativity was unsatisfactory, while a theory which from the outset prefers no state of motion (even accelerated ones) should appear more satisfactory. So in 1908 he published an article on acceleration under special relativity. In that article, he argued that free fall is really inertial motion, and that for a freefalling observer the rules of special relativity must apply. This argument is called the Equivalence principle. In the same article, Einstein also predicted the phenomenon of gravitational time dilation. In 1911, Einstein published another article expanding on the 1907 article, in which additional effects such as the deflection of light by massive bodies were predicted.

General relativity (GR) is a theory of gravitation that was developed by Albert Einstein between 1907 and 1915.

According to general relativity, the observed gravitational attraction between masses results from the warping of space and time by those masses.

Before the advent of general relativity, Newton's law of universal gravitation had been accepted for more than two hundred years as a valid description of the gravitional force between masses, even though Newton himself did not regard the theory as the final word on the nature of gravity. Within a century of Newton's formulation, careful astronomical observation revealed unexplainable variations between the theory and the observations. Under Newton's model, gravity was the result of an attractive force between massive objects. Although even Newton was bothered by the unknown nature of that force, the basic framework was extremely successful at describing motion.

However, experiments and observations show that Einstein's description accounts for several effects that are unexplained by Newton's law, such as minute anomalies in the orbits of Mercury and other planets. General relativity also predicts novel effects of gravity, such as gravitational waves, gravitational lensing and an effect of gravity on time known as gravitational time dilation. Many of these predictions have been confirmed by experiment, while others are the subject of ongoing research. For example, although there is indirect evidence for gravitational waves, direct evidence of their existence is still being sought by several teams of scientists in experiments such as the LIGO and GEO 600 projects.

General relativity has developed into an essential tool in modern astrophysics. It provides the foundation for the current understanding of black holes, regions of space where gravitational attraction is so strong that not even light can escape. Their strong gravity is thought to be responsible for the intense radiation emitted by certain types of astronomical objects (such as active galactic nuclei or microquasars). General relativity is also part of the framework of the standard Big Bang model of cosmology.

General covariance and the hole argument

By 1912, Einstein was actively seeking a theory in which gravitation was explained as a geometric phenomenon. At the urging of Tullio Levi-Civita, Einstein began by exploring the use of general covariance (which is essentially the use of curvature tensors) to create a gravitational theory. However, in 1913 Einstein abandoned that approach, arguing that it is inconsistent based on the "hole argument". In 1914 and much of 1915, Einstein was trying to create field equations based on another approach. When that approach was proven to be inconsistent, Einstein revisited the concept of general covariance and discovered that the hole argument was flawed.

The development of the Einstein Field Equations

When Einstein realized that general covariance was actually tenable, he quickly completed the development of the field equations that are named after him. However, he made a now-famous mistake. The field equations he published in October 1915 were

$$R_{\mu\nu} = T_{\mu\nu},$$

where Rmn is the Ricci tensor, and Tmn the energy-momentum tensor. This predicted the non-Newtonian perihelion precession of Mercury, and so had Einstein very excited. However, it was soon realized that they were inconsistent with the local conservation of energy-momentum unless the universe had a constant density of mass-energy-momentum. In other words, air, rock and even a vacuum should all have the same density. This inconsistency with observation sent Einstein back to the drawing board. However, the solution was all but obvious, and in November 1915 Einstein published the actual Einstein field equations:

$$R_{\mu\nu} - \frac{1}{2} R g_{\mu\nu} = T_{\mu\nu},$$

where *R* is the Ricci scalar and gmn the metric tensor. With the publication of the field equations, the issue became one of solving them for various cases and interpreting the solutions. This and experimental verification have dominated general relativity research ever since.

Einstein and Hilbert

Although Einstein is credited with finding the field equations, the German mathematician David Hilbert published them in an article before Einstein's article. This has resulted in accusations of plagiarism against Einstein (never from Hilbert), and assertions that the field equations should be called the "Einstein-Hilbert field equations". However, Hilbert did not press his claim for priority and some have asserted that Einstein submitted the correct equations before Hilbert amended his own work to include them. This suggests that Einstein developed the correct field equations first, though Hilbert may have reached them later independently (or even learned of them afterwards through his correspondence with Einstein). However, others have criticized those assertions.

Sir Arthur Eddington

In the early years after Einstein's theory was published, Sir Arthur Eddington lent his considerable prestige in the British scientific establishment in an effort to champion the work of this German scientist. Because the theory was so complex and abstruse (even today it is popularly considered the pinnacle of scientific thinking; in the early years it was even more so), it was rumored that only three people in the world understood it. There was an illuminating, though probably apocryphal, anecdote about this. As related by Ludwik Silberstein, during one of Eddington's lectures he asked "Professor Eddington, you must be one of three persons in the world who understands general relativity." Eddington paused, unable to answer. Silberstein continued "Don't be modest, Eddington!" Finally, Eddington replied "On the contrary, I'm trying to think who the third person is."

Solutions

The Schwarzschild solution

Since the field equations are non-linear, Einstein assumed that they were insoluble. However, in 1916 Karl Schwarzschild discovered an exact solution for the case of a spherically symmetric spacetime surrounding a massive object in spherical coordinates. This is now known as the Schwarzschild solution. Since then, many other exact solutions have been found.

The expanding universe and the cosmological constant

In 1922, Alexander Friedmann found a solution in which the universe may expand or contract, and later Georges Lemaître derived a solution for an expanding universe. However, Einstein believed that the universe was apparently static, and since a static cosmology was not supported by the general relativistic field equations, he added a cosmological constant Λ to the field equations, which became

$$R_{\mu\nu} - \frac{1}{2} R g_{\mu\nu} + \Lambda g_{\mu\nu} = T_{\mu\nu} \cdot$$

This permitted the creation of steady-state solutions, but they were unstable: the slightest perturbation of a static state would result in the universe expanding or contracting. In 1929, Edwin Hubble found evidence for the idea that the universe is expanding. This resulted in Einstein dropping the cosmological constant, referring to it as "the biggest blunder in my career". At the time, it was an ad hoc hypothesis to add in the cosmological constant, as it was only intended to justify one result (a static universe).

More exact solutions

Progress in solving the field equations and understanding the solutions has been ongoing. The solution for a spherically symmetric charged object was discovered by Reissner and later rediscovered by Nordström, and is called the Reissner-Nordström solution. The black hole aspect of the Schwarzschild solution was very controversial, and Einstein did not believe that singularities could be real. However, in 1957 (two years after Einstein's death in 1955), Martin Kruskal published a proof that black holes are called for by the Schwarzschild Solution. Additionally, the solution for a rotating massive object was obtained by Kerr in the 1960s and is called the Kerr solution. The Kerr-Newman solution for a rotating, charged massive object was published a few years later.

Testing the theory

The perihelion precession of Mercury was the first evidence that general relativity is correct. Sir Arthur Stanley Eddington's 1919 expedition in which he confirmed Einstein's prediction for the deflection of light by the Sun during the total solar eclipse of May 29, 1919 helped to cement the status of general relativity as a likely true theory.

Since then many observations have confirmed the correctness of general relativity. These include studies of binary pulsars, observations of radio signals passing the limb of the Sun, and even the GPS system. For more information, see the Tests of general relativity article.

Cosmology

In 1917, Einstein applied the General theory of relativity to model the structure of the universe as a whole. He wanted the universe to be eternal and unchanging, but this type of universe is not consistent with relativity. To fix this, Einstein modified the general theory by introducing a new notion, the cosmological constant. With a positive cosmological constant, the universe could be an eternal static sphere

Einstein believed a spherical static universe is philosophically preferred, because it would obey Mach's principle. He had shown that general relativity incorporates Mach's principle to a certain extent in frame dragging by gravitomagnetic fields, but he knew that Mach's idea would not work if space goes on forever. In a closed universe, he believed that Mach's principle would hold.

Mach's principle has generated much controversy over the years.

Modern Quantum Theory

In 1917, at the height of his work on relativity, Einstein published an article in *Physikalische Zeitschrift* that proposed the possibility of stimulated emission, the physical process that makes possible the maser and the laser. This article showed that the statistics of absorption and emission of light would only be consistent with Planck's distribution law if the emission of light into a mode with N photons would be enhanced statistically compared to the emission of light into an empty mode. This paper was enormously influential in the later development of quantum mechanics, because it was the first paper to show that the statistics of atomic transitions had simple laws. Einstein discovered Louis de Broglie's work, and supported his ideas, which were received skeptically at first. In another major paper from this era, Einstein gave a wave equation for de Broglie waves, which Einstein suggested was the Hamilton-Jacobi equation of mechanics. This paper would inspire Schrödinger's work of 1926.

Schrödinger Wave Equation

In 1925, building on De Broglie's theoretical model of particles as waves, Erwin Schrödinger analyzed how an electron would behave if it were assumed to be a wave surrounding a nucleus. Rather than explaining the atom by an analogy to satellites orbiting a planet, he treated electrons as waves with each electron having a unique wavefunction. The mathematical wavefunction is called the "Schrödinger equation" after its creator. Schrödinger's equation describes a wavefunction by three properties (Wolfgang Pauli later added a fourth: spin):

1. An "orbital" designation, indicating whether the particle wave is one that is closer to the nucleus with less energy or one that is farther from the nucleus with more energy;
2. The "shape" of the orbital, spherical or otherwise;
3. The "inclination" of the orbital, determining the magnetic moment of the orbital around the *Z*-axis.

The collective name for these three properties is the "wavefunction of the electron," describing the quantum state of the electron. The quantum state of an electron refers to its collective properties, which describe what can be said about the electron at a point in time. The quantum state of the electron is described by its wavefunction, denoted by the Greek letter ψ ("psi," pronounced "sigh").

The three properties of Schrödinger's equation describing the wavefunction of the electron (and thus its quantum state) are each called quantum numbers. The first property describing the orbital is the principal quantum number, numbered according to Bohr's model, in which *n* denotes the energy of each orbital.

The next quantum number, the azimuthal quantum number, denoted *l* (lower case L), describes the shape of the orbital. The shape is a consequence of the angular momentum of the orbital. The angular momentum represents the resistance of a spinning object to speeding up or slowing down under the influence of external force. The azimuthal quantum number *l* represents the orbital angular momentum of an electron around its nucleus. However, the shape of each orbital has its own letter as well. The first shape is denoted by the letter *s* (for "spherical"). The next shape is denoted by the letter *p* and has the form of a dumbbell. The other orbitals have more complicated shapes, and are denoted by the letters *d*, *f*, and *g*.

The third quantum number in Schrödinger's equation describes the magnetic moment of the electron. This number is denoted by either *m* or *m* with a subscript *l*, because the magnetic moment depends on the second quantum number *l*.

In May 1926, Schrödinger proved that Heisenberg's matrix mechanics and his own wave mechanics made the same predictions about the properties and behaviour of the electron; mathematically, the two theories were identical. Yet both men disagreed on the physical interpretations of their respective theories. Heisenberg saw no problem in the existence of discontinuous quantum jumps, while

Schrödinger hoped that a theory based on continuous wave-like properties could avoid what he called (in the words of Wilhelm Wien), "this nonsense about quantum jumps."

Bose-Einstein Condensate

A Bose-Einstein condensate (BEC) is a state of matter of a dilute gas of weakly interacting bosons confined in an external potential and cooled to temperatures very near to absolute zero (0 K, -273.15 °C, or -459.67 °F). Under such conditions, a large fraction of the bosons occupy the lowest quantum state of the external potential, and all wave functions overlap each other, at which point quantum effects become apparent on a macroscopic scale.

This state of matter was first predicted by Satyendra Nath Bose and Albert Einstein in 1924-25. Bose first sent a paper to Einstein on the quantum statistics of light quanta (now called photons). Einstein was impressed, translated the paper himself from English to German and submitted it for Bose to the Zeitschrift für Physik which published it. Einstein then extended Bose's ideas to material particles (or matter) in two other papers.

Seventy years later, the first gaseous condensate was produced by Eric Cornell and Carl Wieman in 1995 at the University of Colourado at Boulder NIST-JILA lab, using a gas of rubidium atoms cooled to 170 nanokelvin (*Nk*) (1.7×10-7 K). For their acheivments Cornell, Wieman, and Wolfgang Ketterle at MIT received the 2001 Nobel Prize in Physics.

Theory

The slowing of atoms by use of cooling apparatus produces a singular quantum state known as a *Bose condensate* or *Bose-Einstein condensate.* This phenomenon was predicted in 1925 by generalizing Satyendra Nath Bose's work on the statistical mechanics of (massless) photons to (massive) atoms. (The Einstein manuscript, once believed to be lost, was found in a library at Leiden University in 2005.) The result of the efforts of Bose and Einstein is the concept of a Bose gas, governed by Bose-Einstein statistics, which describes the statistical distribution of identical particles with integer spin, now known as bosons. Bosonic particles, which include the photon as well as atoms such as helium-4, are allowed to share quantum states with each other. Einstein demonstrated that cooling bosonic atoms to a very low temperature would cause them to fall (or "condense") into the lowest accessible quantum state, resulting in a new form of matter.

This transition occurs below a critical temperature, which for a uniform three-dimensional gas consisting of non-interacting particles with no apparent internal degrees of freedom is given by:

$$T_c = \left(\frac{n}{\zeta(3/2)}\right)^{2/3} \frac{2\pi\hbar^2}{mk_B} \approx 3.3125 \frac{\hbar^2 n^{2/3}}{mk_B}$$

where:

T_c is the critical temperature,

n is the particle density,

m is the mass per boson,

$\hbar$ is the reduced Planck constant,

k_B is the Boltzmann constant,

and ζ is the Riemann zeta function;

$\zeta(3/2) \approx 2.6124$.

(sequence A078434 in OEIS)

Einstein's argument

Consider a collection of N noninteracting particles which can each be in one of two quantum states, $|0\rangle$ and $|1\rangle$. If the two states are equal in energy, each different configuration is equally likely.

If we can tell which particle is which, there are 2^N different configurations, since each particle can be in $|0\rangle$ or $|1\rangle$ independently. In almost all the configurations, about half the particles are in $|0\rangle$ and the other half in $|1\rangle$. The balance is a statistical effect, the number of configurations is largest when the particles are divided equally.

If the particles are indistinguishable, however, there are only $N + 1$ different configurations. If there are K particles in state $|1\rangle$, there are N-K particles in state $|0\rangle$. Whether any particular particle is in state $|0\rangle$ or in state $|1\rangle$ cannot be determined, so each value of K determines a unique quantum state for the whole system. If all these states are equally likely, there is no statistical spreading out; it is just as likely for all the particles to sit in $|0\rangle$ as for the particles to be split half and half.

Suppose now that the energy of state $|1\rangle$ is slightly greater than the energy of state $|0\rangle$ by an amount E. At temperature T, a particle will have a lesser probability to be in state $|1\rangle$ by $\exp(-E/T)$. In the distinguishable case, the particle distribution will be biased slightly towards state $|0\rangle$ and the distribution will be slightly different from half and half. But in the indistinguishable case, since there is no statistical pressure toward equal numbers, the most likely outcome is that most of the particles will collapse into state $|0\rangle$.

In the distinguishable case, for large N, the fraction in state $|0\rangle$ can be computed. It is the same as coin flipping with a coin which has probability $p = exp(-E/T)$ to land tails. The fraction of heads is $1/(1+p)$, which is a smooth function of p, of the energy.

In the indistinguishable case, each value of K is a single state, which has its own separate Boltzmann probability. So the probability distribution is exponential:

$$P(K) = Ce^{-KE/T} = Cp^{K}.$$

For large N, the normalization constant C is $(1-p)$. The expected total number of particles which are not in the lowest energy state, in the limit that $N \to \infty$, is equal to :

$$\sum_{n>0} Cnp^n = p/(1-p).$$

It doesn't grow when N is large, it just approaches a constant. This will be a negligible fraction of the total number of particles. So a collection of enough Bose particles in thermal equilibrium will mostly be in the ground state, with only a few in any excited state, no matter how small the energy difference.

Consider now a gas of particles, which can be in different momentum states labelled $|k\rangle$. If the number of particles is less than the number of thermally accessible states, for high temperatures and low densities, the particles will all be in different states. In this limit the gas is classical. As the density increases or the temperature decreases, the number of accessible states pe: particle becomes smaller, and at some point more particles will be forced into a single state than the maximum allowed for that state by statistical weighting. From this point on, any extra particle added will go into the ground state.

To calculate the transition temperature at any density, integrate over all momentum states the expression for maximum number of excited particles *p/(1-p)*:

$$N = V\int \frac{d^3k}{(2\pi)^3} \frac{p(k)}{1-p(k)} = V\int \frac{d^3k}{(2\pi)^3} \frac{1}{e^{\frac{k^2}{2mT}}-1}$$

$$p(k) = e^{\frac{-k^2}{2mT}}.$$

When the integral is evaluated with the factors of k_B and $\hbar$ restored by dimensional analysis, it gives the critical temperature formula of the preceding section. Therefore, this integral defines the critical temperature and particle number corresponding to the conditions of zero chemical potential ($\mu = 0$ in the Bose-Einstein statistics distribution).

Gross-Pitaevskii Equation

The state of the BEC can be described by the wavefunction of the condensate $\psi(\vec{r})$. For a system of this nature, $|\psi(\vec{r})|^2$ is interpreted as the particle density, so the total number of atoms is

$$N = \int d\vec{r}\, |\psi(\vec{r})|^2$$

Provided essentially all atoms are in the condensate (that is, have condensed to the ground state), and treating the bosons using mean field theory, the energy (E) associated with the state $\psi(\vec{r})$ is:

$(\vec{r})|^2$

$$E = \int d\vec{r} \left[\frac{\hbar^2}{2m} |\nabla\psi(\vec{r})|^2 + V(\vec{r})\,|\psi(\vec{r})|^2 + \frac{1}{2}U_0\,|\psi(\vec{r})|^4 \right]$$

Minimising this energy with respect to infinitesimal variations in $\psi(\vec{r})$, and holding the number of atoms constant, yields the Gross-Pitaevski equation (GPE) (also a non-linear Schrödinger equation):

$$i\hbar \frac{\partial\psi(\vec{r})}{\partial t} = \left(-\frac{\hbar^2\nabla^2}{2m} + V(\vec{r}) + U_0\,|\psi(\vec{r})|^2 \right)\psi(\vec{r})$$

where:

m is the mass of the bosons,

V(r) is the external potential,

Uq is representative of the inter-particle interactions.

The GPE provides a good description of the behaviour of BEC's and is thus often applied for theoretical analysis.

Discovery

In 1938, Pyotr Kapitsa, John Allen and Don Misener discovered that helium-4 became a new kind of fluid, now known as a superfluid, at temperatures less than 2.17 K (the lambda point). Superfluid helium has many unusual properties, including zero viscosity (the ability to flow without dissipating energy) and the existence of quantized vortices. It was quickly realized that the superfluidity was due to partial Bose-Einstein condensation of the liquid. In fact, many of the properties of superfluid helium also appear in the gaseous Bose-Einstein condensates created by Cornell, Wieman and Ketterle (see below). Superfluid helium-4 is a liquid rather than a gas, which means that the interactions between the atoms are relatively strong; the original theory of Bose-Einstein condensation must be heavily modified in order to describe it. Bose-Einstein condensation remains, however, fundamental to the superfluid properties of helium-4. Note that helium-3, consisting of fermions instead of bosons, also enters a superfluid phase at low temperature, which can be explained by the formation of bosonic Cooper pairs of two atoms each.

The first "pure" Bose-Einstein condensate was created by Eric Cornell, Carl Wieman, and co-workers at JILA on June 5, 1995. They did this by cooling a dilute vapor consisting of approximately two thousand rubidium-87 atoms to below 170 *Nk* using a combination of laser cooling (a technique that won its inventors Steven Chu, Claude Cohen-Tannoudji, and William D. Phillips the 1997 Nobel Prize in Physics) and magnetic evaporative cooling. About four months later, an independent effort led by Wolfgang Ketterle at MIT created a condensate made of sodium-23. Ketterle's condensate had about a hundred times more atoms, allowing him to obtain several important results such as the observation of quantum mechanical interference between two different condensates. Cornell, Wieman and Ketterle won the 2001 Nobel Prize in Physics for their achievement.

The Bose-Einstein condensation also applies to quasiparticles in solids. A magnon in an antiferromagnet carries spin 1 and thus obeys Bose-Einstein statistics. The density of magnons is controlled by an external magnetic field, which plays the role of the magnon chemical potential. This technique provides access to a wide range of boson densities from the limit of a dilute Bose gas to that of a strongly interacting Bose liquid. A magnetic ordering observed at the point of condensation is the analog of superfluidity. In 1999 Bose condensation of magnons was demonstrated in the antiferromagnet TlCuCl3. The condensation was observed at temperatures as large as 14 K.

Such a high transition temperature (relative to that of atomic gases) is due to the greater density achievable with magnons and the smaller mass (roughly equal to the mass of an electron). In 2006, condensation of magnons in ferromagnets was even shown at room temperature, where the authors used pumping techniques.

Vortices

As in many other systems, vortices can exist in BECs. These can be created, for example, by 'stirring' the condensate with lasers, or rotating the confining trap. The vortex created will be a quantum vortex. These phenomena are allowed for by the non-linear $|\psi(\vec{r})|^2$ term in the GPE. As the vortices must have quantised angular momentum, the wavefunction will be of the form $\psi(\vec{r}) = \phi(\rho, z)e^{i\ell\theta}$ where ρ, Z and θ are as in the cylindrical coordinate system, and ℓ is the angular number. To determine $\varphi(\rho, Z)$, the energy of must be minimised, according to the constraint $\psi(\vec{r})$. This is usually done computationally, however in a uniform medium the analytic form

$$\phi = \frac{nx}{\sqrt{2+x^2}}$$

where:

n^2 is density far from the vortex,

$$x = \frac{\rho}{\ell\xi},$$

ξ is healing length of the condensate.

demonstrates the correct behaviour, and is a good approximation.

A singly-charged vortex () is in the ground state, with its energy ε_v given by

$$\epsilon_v = \pi n \frac{\hbar^2}{m} \ln\left(1.464 \frac{b}{\xi}\right)$$

where:

b is the farthest distance from the vortex considered.

(To obtain an energy which is well defined it is necessary to include this boundary b.)

For multiply-charged vortices $(\ell > 1)$ the energy is approximated by

$$\epsilon_v \approx \ell^2 \pi n \frac{\hbar^2}{m} \ln\left(\frac{b}{\xi}\right)$$

which is greater than that of ℓ singly-charged vortices, indicating that these multiply-charged vortices are unstable to decay. Research has, however, indicated they are metastable states, so may have relatively long lifetimes.

Closely related to the creation of vortices in BECs is the generation of so-called dark solitons in one-dimensional BECs. These topological objects feature a phase gradient across their nodal plane, which stabilizes their shape even in propagation and interaction. Although solitons carry no charge and are thus prone to decay, relatively long-lived dark solitons have been produced and studied extensively.

Unusual characteristics

Further experimentation by the JILA team in 2000 uncovered a hitherto unknown property of Bose-Einstein condensates. Cornell, Wieman, and their coworkers originally used rubidium-87, an isotope whose atoms naturally repel each other, making a more stable condensate. The JILA team instrumentation now had better control over the condensate so experimentation was made on naturally attracting atoms of another rubidium isotope, rubidium-85 (having negative atom-atom scattering length). Through a process called Feshbach resonance involving a sweep of the magnetic field causing spin flip collisions, the JILA researchers lowered the characteristic, discrete energies at which the rubidium atoms bond into molecules, making their Rb-85 atoms repulsive and creating a stable condensate. The reversible flip from attraction to repulsion stems from quantum interference among condensate atoms which behave as waves.

When the scientists raised the magnetic field strength still further, the condensate suddenly reverted back to attraction, imploded and shrank beyond detection, and then exploded, blowing off about two-thirds of its 10,000 or so atoms. About half of the atoms in the condensate seemed to have disappeared from the experiment altogether, not being seen either in the cold remnant or the expanding gas cloud. Carl Wieman explained that under current atomic theory this characteristic of Bose-Einstein condensate could not be explained because the energy state of an atom near absolute zero should not be enough to cause an implosion; however, subsequent mean field theories have been proposed to explain it.

Because supernova explosions are also preceded by an implosion, the explosion of a collapsing Bose-Einstein condensate was named "bosenova", a pun on the musical style bossa nova.

The atoms that seem to have disappeared almost certainly still exist in some form, just not in a form that could be accounted for in that experiment. Most likely they formed molecules consisting of two bonded rubidium atoms. The energy gained by making this transition imparts a velocity sufficient for them to leave the trap without being detected.

Current research

Compared to more commonly encountered states of matter, Bose-Einstein condensates are extremely fragile. The slightest interaction with the outside world can be enough to warm them past the condensation threshold, eliminating their interesting properties and forming a normal gas. It is likely to be some time before any practical applications are developed.

Nevertheless, they have proven useful in exploring a wide range of questions in fundamental physics, and the years since the initial discoveries by the JILA and MIT groups have seen an explosion in experimental and theoretical activity. Examples include experiments that have demonstrated interference between condensates due to wave-particle duality, the study of superfluidity and quantized vortices, and the slowing of light pulses to very low speeds using electromagnetically induced transparency. Vortices in Bose-Einstein condensates are also currently the subject of analogue gravity research, studying the possibility of modeling black holes and their related phenomena in such environments in the lab. Experimentalists have also realized "optical lattices", where the interference pattern from overlapping lasers provides a periodic potential for the condensate. These have been used to explore the transition between a superfluid and a Mott insulator, and may be useful in studying Bose-Einstein condensation in fewer than three dimensions, for example the Tonks-Girardeau gas.

Bose-Einstein condensates composed of a wide range of isotopes have been produced.

Related experiments in cooling fermions rather than bosons to extremely low temperatures have created degenerate gases, where the atoms do not congregate in a single state due to the Pauli exclusion principle. To exhibit Bose-Einstein condensation, the fermions must "pair up" to form compound particles (e.g. molecules or Cooper pairs) that are bosons. The first molecular Bose-Einstein condensates were created in November 2003 by the groups of

Rudolf Grimm at the University of Innsbruck, Deborah S. Jin at the University of Colourado at Boulder and Wolfgang Ketterle at MIT. Jin quickly went on to create the first fermionic condensate composed of Cooper pairs.

In 1999, Danish physicist Lene Vestergaard Hau led a team from Harvard University which succeeded in slowing a beam of light to about 17 metres per second and, in 2001, was able to momentarily stop a beam. She was able to achieve this by using a superfluid. Hau and her associates at Harvard University have since successfully transformed light into matter and back into light using Bose-Einstein condensates: details of the experiment are discussed in an article in the journal Nature, 8 February 2007.

Subtleties

Up to 2004, using the above-mentioned "ultralow temperatures", Bose-Einstein condensates had been obtained for a multitude of isotopes involving mainly alkaline and alkaline earth atoms (^{7}Li, ^{23}Na, ^{41}K, ^{52}Cr, ^{84}St, ^{85}Rb, ^{87}Rb, ^{133}Cs and ^{174}Yb). Not astonishingly, condensation research was finally successful even with hydrogen, although with the aid of special methods. In contrast, the superfluid state of the bosonic 4He at temperatures below the temperature of 2.17 K is *not* a good example of Bose-Einstein condensation, because the interaction between the 4He bosons is simply too strong, so that at zero temperature, contrary to Bose-Einstein theory, only 8% rather than 100% of the atoms are in the ground state. Even the fact that the above-mentioned alkaline gases show bosonic, rather than fermionic behaviour, as solid state physicists or chemists would expect, is based on a subtle interplay of electronic and nuclear spins: at ultralow temperatures and corresponding excitation energies, the half-integer (in units of $\hbar$) total spin of the electronic shell and the also half-integer total spin of the nucleus of the atom are coupled by the (very weak) hyperfine interaction to the integer (!) total spin of the atom. Only the fact that this last-mentioned total spin is integral causes the ultralow-temperature behaviour of the atom to be bosonic, whereas the "chemistry" of the systems at room temperature is determined by the electronic properties, i.e. is essentially fermionic, since at room temperature thermal excitations have typical energies which are much higher than the hyperfine values. (Here one should remember the spin-statistics theorem of Wolfgang Pauli, which states that half-integer spins lead to fermionic behaviour, e.g., the Pauli exclusion principle forbidding that more than two electrons possess the same energy, whereas integer spins lead to bosonic behaviour, e.g., condensation of identical bosonic particles in a common ground state.)

The ultralow temperature requirement of Bose-Einstein condensates of alkali metals does not generalize to all types of

Bose-Einstein condensates. In 2006, physicists under S. Demokritov in Münster, Germany, found Bose-Einstein condensation of magnons (i.e. quantized spinwaves) at room temperature, admittedly by the application of pump processes.

Energy Momentum Pseudotensor

In the theory of general relativity, a stress-energy-momentum pseudotensor, such as the Landau-Lifshitz pseudotensor, is an extension of the non-gravitational stress-energy tensor which incorporates the energy-momentum of gravity. It allows the energy-momentum of a system of gravitating matter to be defined. In particular it allows the total of matter plus the gravitating energy-momentum to form a conserved current within the framework of general relativity, so that the total energy-momentum crossing the hypersurface (3-dimensional boundary) of any compact space-time hypervolume (4-dimensional submanifold) vanishes.

Some people object to this derivation on the grounds that pseudotensors are inappropriate objects in general relativity, but the conservation law only requires the use of the 4-divergence of a pseudotensor which is, in this case, a tensor (which also vanishes). Also, most pseudotensors are sections of jet bundles, which are perfectly valid objects in GR.

General relativity includes a dynamical spacetime, so it is difficult to see how to identify the conserved energy and momentum. Noether's theorem allows these quantities to be determined from a Lagrangian with translation invariance, but general covariance makes translation invariance into something of a gauge symmetry. The energy and momentum derived within general relativity by Noether's presecriptions do not make a real tensor for this reason.

Einstein argued that this is true for fundamental reasons, because the gravitational field could be made to vanish by a choice of coordinates. He maintained that the non-covariant energy momentum pseudotensor was in fact the best description of the energy momentum distribution in a gravitational field. This approach has been echoed by Lev Landau and Evgeny Lifshitz, and others, and has become standard.

The use of non-covariant objects like pseudotensors was heavily criticized in 1917 by Erwin Schrödinger and others.

Unified Field Theories

Since the 1800s, some physicists have attempted to develop a single theoretical framework that can account for the fundamental forces of nature — a unified field theory. Classical unified field theories are attempts to create a unified field theory based on classical physics. In particular, unification of gravitation and electromagnetism was actively pursued by several physicists and mathematicians in the years between World War I and World War II. This work spurred the purely mathematical development of differential geometry. Albert Einstein is the best known of the many physicists who attempted to develop a classical unified field theory.

Overview

The early attempts at creating a unified field theory began with the Riemannian geometry of general relativity, and attempted to incorporate electromagnetic fields into a more general geometry, since ordinary Riemannian geometry seemed incapable of expressing the properties of the electromagnetic field. Einstein was not alone in his attempts to unify electromagnetism and gravity; a large number of mathematicians and physicists, including Hermann Weyl, Arthur Eddington, Theodor Kaluza, Lancelot Law Whyte, and R. Bach also attempted to develop approaches that could unify these interactions. These scientists pursued several avenues of generalization, including extending the foundations of geometry and adding an extra spatial dimension.

Early work

The first attempts to provide a unified theory were by G. Mie in 1912 and Ernst Reichenbacher in 1916. However, these theories were unsatisfactory, as they did not incorporate general relativity — in the former case, because general relativity had yet to be formulated. These efforts, along with those of Forster, involved making the metric tensor (which had previously been assumed to be symmetric and real-valued) into an asymmetric and/or compleX-valued tensor, and they also attempted to create a field theory for matter as well.

Differential geometry and field theory

From 1918 until 1923, there were four distinct approaches to field theory: the gauge theory of Weyl, Kaluza's five-dimensional theory, Lancelot Law Whyte's theory based on the Unitary Principle and Eddington's development of affine geometry. Einstein corresponded with these researchers, and collaborated with Kaluza, but was not yet fully involved in the unification effort.

Weyl's infinitesimal geometry

In order to include electromagnetism into the geometry of general relativity, Hermann Weyl worked to generalize the Riemannian geometry upon which general relativity is based. His idea was to create a more general infinitesimal geometry. He noted that in addition to a metric field there could be additional degrees of freedom along a path between two points in a manifold, and he tried to exploit this by introducing a basic method for comparison of local size measures along such a path, in terms of a gauge field. This geometry generalized Riemannian geometry in that there was a vector field *Q*, in addition to the metric g, which together gave rise to both the electromagnetic and gravitational fields. This theory was mathematically sound, albeit complicated, resulting in difficult and high-order field equations. The critical mathematical ingredients in this theory, the Lagrangians and curvature tensor, were worked out by Weyl and colleagues. Then Weyl carried out an extensive correspondence with Einstein and others as to its physical validity, and the theory was ultimately found to be physically unreasonable. However, Weyl's principle of gauge invariance was later applied in a modified form to quantum field theory.

Kaluza's fifth dimension

Kaluza's approach to unification was to embed space-time into a five-dimensional cylindrical world; one of four space dimensions and one of time. Unlike Weyl's approach, Riemannian geometry was maintained, and the extra dimension allowed for the incorporation of the electromagnetic field vector into the geometry. Despite the relative mathematical elegance of this approach, in collaboration with Einstein and Einstein's aide Grommer it was determined that this theory did not admit a non-singular, static, spherically symmetric solution. This theory did have some influence on Einstein's later work and was further developed later by Klein in an attempt to incorporate relativity into quantum theory, in what is now known as Kaluza-Klein theory.

Lancelot Law Whyte's unitary field theory

This theory was based on an organizing process called by Lancelot Law Whyte the "Unitary Principle". The history of this theoretical approach is: Michael Faraday and James Clerk Maxwell worked from Rudjer Boscovich's theory, which dealt with non-Euclidean and higher-dimensional geometry. This prompted mathematicians such as Gauss and Riemann to investigate that area of mathematics. The mathematics that Riemann developed was used by Einstein in his theory of general relativity, but that was not as extensive a description as Boscovich's theory, for which the mathematics had been only incompletely developed. Lancelot Law Whyte's ideas were adopted for experimental work by Leo Baranski, who planned a series of books based upon this theory. Only Baranski's first book was published before his untimely death, upon which this line of investigation based upon classical physics was abandoned by academia.

Eddington's affine geometry

Sir Arthur Stanley Eddington was a noted astronomer who became an enthusiastic and influential promoter of Einstein's general theory of relativity. He was among the first to propose an extension of the gravitational theory based on the affine connection as the fundamental structure field rather than the metric tensor which was the original focus of general relativity. Affine connection is the basis for *parallel transport* of vectors from one space-time point to another; Eddington assumed the affine connection to be symmetric in its covariant indices, because it seemed plausible that the result of parallel-transporting one infinitesimal vector along another should produce the same result as transporting the second along the first. (Later workers revisited this assumption.)

Eddington emphasized what he considered to be epistemological considerations; for example, he thought that the cosmological constant version of the general-relativistic field equation expressed the property that the universe was "self-gauging". Since the simpiest cosmological model (the De Sitter universe) that solves that equation is a spherically symmetric, stationary, closed universe (exhibiting a cosmological red shift, which is more conventionally interpreted as due to expansion), it seemed to explain the overall form of the universe.

Like many other classical unified field theorists, Eddington considered that in the Einstein field equations for general relativity the stress-energy tensor $T\mu\nu$, which represents matter/energy, was merely provisional, and that in a truly unified theory the source term would automatically arise as some aspect of the free-space field equations. He also shared the hope that an improved fundamental theory would explain why the two elementary particles then known (proton and electron) have quite different masses.

The Dirac equation for the relativistic quantum electron caused Eddington to rethink his previous conviction that fundamental physical theory had to be based on tensors. He subsequently devoted his efforts into development of a "Fundamental Theory" based largely on algebraic notions (which he called "E-frames"). Unfortunately his descriptions of this theory were sketchy and difficult to understand, so very few physicists followed up on his work.

Einstein's geometric approaches

When the equivalent of Maxwell's equations for electromagnetism is formulated within the framework of Einstein's theory of general relativity, the electromagnetic field energy (being equivalent to mass as one would expect from Einstein's famous equation $E=mc^2$) contributes to the stress tensor and thus to the curvature of space-time, which is the general-relativistic representation of the gravitational field; or putting it another way, certain configurations of curved space-time *incorporate* effects of an electromagnetic field. This suggests that a purely geometric theory ought to treat these two fields as different aspects of the same basic phenomenon. However, ordinary Riemannian geometry is unable to describe the properties of the electromagnetic field as a purely geometric phenomenon.

Einstein tried to form a generalized theory of gravitation that would unify the gravitational and electromagnetic forces (and perhaps others), guided by a belief in a single origin for the entire set of physical laws. These attempts initially concentrated on additional geometric notions such as vierbeins and "distant parallelism", but eventually centered around treating both the metric tensor and the affine connection as fundamental fields. (Because they are not independent, the metric-affine theory was somewhat complicated.) In general relativity, these fields are symmetric (in the matrix sense), but since antisymmetry seemed essential for electromagnetism, the symmetry requirement was relaxed for one or both fields. Einstein's proposed unified-field equations (fundamental laws of physics) were generally derived from a variational principle expressed in terms of the Riemann curvature tensor for the presumed space-time manifold.

In field theories of this kind, particles appear as limited regions in space-time in which the field strength or the energy density are particularly high. Einstein and coworker Leopold Infeld managed to demonstrate that, in Einstein's final theory of the unified field, true singularities of the field did have trajectories resembling point particles. However, singularities are places where the equations break down, and Einstein believed that in an ultimate theory the laws should apply *everywhere*, with particles being soliton-like solutions to the (highly nonlinear) field equations. Further, the large-scale topology of the universe should impose restrictions on the solutions, such as quantization or discrete symmetries.

The degree of abstraction, combined with a relative lack of good mathematical tools for analyzing nonlinear equation systems, make it hard to connect such theories with the physical phenomena that they might describe. For example, it has been suggested that the torsion (antisymmetric part of the affine connection) might be related to isospin rather than electromagnetism; this is related to a discrete (or "*internal*") symmetry known to Einstein as "displacement field duality".

Einstein became increasingly isolated in his research on a generalized theory of gravitation, and most physicists consider his attempts ultimately unsuccessful. In particular, his pursuit of a unification of the fundamental forces ignored developments in quantum physics (and vice versa), most notably the discovery of the strong nuclear force and weak nuclear force. Recent work by Komech (A.I.Komech, Lectures on Quantum Mechanics (nonlinear PDE point of view), http://arxiv.org/PS_cache/math-ph/pdf/0505/0505059v4.pdf) puts Einstein's earlier work in a more favorable light. This book realizes Einstein's Unified Field Theory Program and shows that almost all the empirical results known until the 1980's were derivable from it. From the quantum mechanical point of view, it is a local hidden variables theory and hence cannot derive EPR type results. EPR type experiments were performed in the 1980's and confirmed quantum theory; leaving viable only Bohmian style non-local hidden variable theories which are not Lorentz invariant. Such applications as quantum cryptography and quantum computing require EPR type situations. The Maxwell-Dirac system is the super-classical limit of (the not mathematically well-defined) QED.

Schrödinger's pure-affine theory

Inspired by Einstein's approach to a unified field theory and Eddington's idea of the affine connection as the sole basis for differential geometric structure for space-time, Erwin Schrödinger from 1940 to 1951 thoroughly investigated pure-affine formulations of generalized gravitational theory. Although he initially assumed a symmetric affine connection, like Einstein he later considered the nonsymmetric field.

Schrödinger's most striking discovery during this work was that the metric tensor was *induced* upon the manifold via a simple construction from the Riemann curvature tensor, which was in turn formed entirely from the affine connection. Further, taking this approach with the simplest feasible basis for the variational principle resulted in a field equation having the form of Einstein's general-relativistic field equation with a cosmological term arising *automatically*.

Skepticism from Einstein and published criticisms from other physicists discouraged Schrödinger, and his work in this area has been largely ignored.

Later work

After the 1930s, progressively fewer scientists worked on classical unification, due to the continual development of quantum theory and the difficulties encountered in developing a quantum theory of gravity. Einstein continued to work on unified field theories of gravity and electromagnetism, but he became increasingly isolated in this research, which he pursued until his death. Despite the publicity of this work due to Einstein's celebrity status, it never resulted in a resounding success.

Most scientists, though not Einstein, eventually abandoned classical theories. Current research on unified field theories focuses on the problem of creating quantum gravity and unifying such a theory with the other fundamental theories in physics, which are quantum theories. (Some programs, most notably string theory, attempt to solve both of these problems at once.) With four fundamental forces now identified, gravity remains the one force whose unification proves problematic.

Wormholes

In physics, a wormhole is a hypothetical topological feature of spacetime that is, fundamentally, a 'shortcut' through space and time. Simply, spacetime is a two-dimensional (2-D) surface that, when 'folded' over, allows the formation of a wormhole bridge. A wormhole has at least two mouths that are connected via a throat or tube. If the wormhole is traversable, then matter can 'travel' from one mouth to the other via the throat. There is no observational evidence for wormholes, and, although wormholes are valid solutions in general relativity, this is only true if exotic matter can be used to stabilize them. Even if the wormhole is stabilized, even a slight fluctuation in space would collapse it. If such exotic matter — that is, matter with negative mass — does not exist, all wormhole-containing solutions to Einstein's field equations are vacuum solutions, which require an impossible vacuum, free of all matter and energy.

The American theoretical physicist John Archibald Wheeler coined the term *wormhole* in 1957; however, in 1921, the German mathematician Hermann Weyl already had proposed the wormhole theory, in connection with mass analysis of electromagnetic field energy.

Einstein collaborated with others to produce a model of a wormhole. His motivation was to model elementary particles with charge as a solution of gravitational field equations, in line with the program outlined in the paper "Do Gravitational Fields play an Important Role in the Constitution of the Elementary Particles?". These solutions cut and pasted Schwarzschild black holes to make a bridge between two patches. If one end of a wormhole was positively charged, the other end would be negatively charged. These properties led Einstein to believe that pairs of particles and antiparticles could be described in this way.

Einstein-Cartan Theory

Einstein-Cartan theory in theoretical physics extends general relativity to correctly handle spin angular momentum. As the master theory of classical physics, general relativity has one known flaw: it cannot describe "spin-orbit coupling", i.e., exchange of intrinsic angular momentum (spin) and orbital angular momentum. There is a qualitative proof showing that general relativity must be extended to Einstein-Cartan theory when matter with spin is present.

Experimental effects are too small to be observed at the present time because the spin tensor of typical macroscopic objects is often small *and* torsion is nonpropagating which means that torsion will only appear *within* a massive body. In addition, only spinning objects couple to torsion. Other sources however describe propagating torsion.

The theory is named after Albert Einstein and Élie Cartan.

Motivation

The reason that general relativity cannot describe spin-orbit coupling is rooted in Riemannian geometry, on which general relativity is based. In Riemannian geometry, the Ricci curvature tensor

R_{ab}

must be symmetric in a and b (that is, $R_{ab} = R_{ba}$). Therefore the Einstein curvature tensor Gab defined as

$$G_{ab} \equiv R_{ab} - \frac{1}{2} R g_{ab}$$

must be symmetric. In general relativity, the Einstein curvature tensor models local gravitational forces, and it is equal (up to a gravitational constant) to the momentum tensor

P_{ab}

(We denote the stress-energy tensor by P because the customary symuol T in general relativity is used in Einstein-Cartan theory to denote affine torsion. The momentum tensor is also called the stress-energy tensor, the energy-momentum tensor, and the energy-momentum-stress tensor. Special relativity shows that energy, momentum, momentum flux, and stress are different spacetime components of the same covariant object, known most compactly as the momentum tensor.)

The symmetry of the Einstein curvature tensor forces the momentum tensor to be symmetric. However, when spin and orbital angular momentum are being exchanged, the momentum tensor is known to be nonsymmetric according to the general equation of conservation of angular momentum

(divergence of spin current) $\propto (P_{ab} \;\; P_{ba}) \neq 0$.

Therefore general relativity cannot properly model spin-orbit coupling.

In 1922 Élie Cartan conjectured that general relativity should be extended by including affine torsion, which allows the Ricci tensor to be non-symmetric. Although spin-orbit coupling is a relatively minor phenomenon in gravitational physics, Einstein-Cartan theory is quite important because:

(1) it makes clear that an affine theory, not a metric theory, provides a better description of gravitation;

(2) it explains the meaning of affine torsion, which appears naturally in some theories of quantum gravity; and

(3) it interprets spin as affine torsion, which geometrically is a continuum approximation to a field of dislocations in the spacetime medium.

The extension of Riemannian geometry to include affine torsion is now known as Riemann-Cartan geometry.

Geometric Foundations

The basic mathematics underlying spacetime physics are the ideas of affine connections and differential geometry, in which we endow an N dimensional differentiable manifold M with a law of parallel translation of vectors along paths in M. (At each point of a differentiable manifold, we have a linear space of tangent vectors, but we have no way to transport vectors to another point, or to compare vectors at two points in M.) The parallel translation preserves linear relationships between vectors; that is, if two vectors u and v at the same point of *M* parallel translate along a curve to vectors u' and v', then

$$a\,u + b\,v$$

parallel translates to a

$$a\,u' + b\,v'.$$

Parallelism is path-dependent; that is, if you parallel translate a vector along two different paths with the same starting and ending points, the resulting vectors at the end point in general differ. The difference between parallel-translating a vector along different curves is the essential meaning of curvature, which is the central concept in differential geometry (and general relativity).

In (pseudo) Riemannian geometry, an *N* dimensional differential manifold *M* is endowed with a Riemannian metric g, which is a nondegenerate linear map that maps two tangent vectors to a real number. The metric uniquely determines a law of parallel translation that preserves inner products between vectors and has zero torsion. This law of parallel translation is called the Levi-Civita connection.

(In the more abstract language of fiber bundles, if the metric *g* is preserved by the connection, then the structure group of the principal bundle is reducible to the orthogonal group O(p,q), where the metric *g* has *p* principal directions with positive length and q principal directions with negative length.)

A Riemann-Cartan geometry is uniquely determined by

- a metric tensor field g that specifies all lengths of vectors and angles between vectors.
- the requirement that lengths and angles are preserved by parallel transport. This is expressed by the condition that the covariant derivative of the metric tensor vanishes:

$$\Delta g = 0$$

where Δ is the covariant derivative determined by the affine connection.

- an affine torsion field Θ

$$\Delta_u V - \Delta_v u - [u,v] = \Theta(u,v)$$

where u and v are vector fields and [,] is the Lie bracket.

In Riemann-Cartan geometry, the curvature tensor has a rotational part

$$R_{klj}^{\ \ \ i}$$

analogous to the curvature in Riemannian geometry, and a translational part, the affine torsion

$$T_{kj}^{\ \ i}.$$

The rotational curvature describes the rotation in the i, j plane experienced by a vector that is parallel translated around a small loop in the k, l plane in the base manifold. The translational curvature $T_{kj}^{\ \ i}$ describes the translation in the K direction resulting from 'developing' a small loop in the i-j plane in the base manifold M into a flat manifold X that has the same dimension as M. (Developing a curve)

$$C_m : [0,1] \rightarrow M$$

into a curve

$$C_x : [0,1] \rightarrow X$$

means defining a curve C_x in *X* that has the same pattern of accelerations as the curve C_m in M. The motivation for development of a curve C_m is to create a curve C_x whose shape is determined by the same pattern of accelerations as Cm, but without the impact on shape of curve C_x from the curvature of the ambient space M.)

A Riemann-Cartan geometry with zero torsion is a Riemannian geometry.

How to include spacetime translations in fiber bundle gauge theories has been a subject of controversy for 50 years, because spacetime symmetries are not internal symmetries of the bundle structure group. A consistent approach to including translations in spacetime theories is outlined in (Petti 2006).

The best way to formulate Einstein-Cartan theory is to distinguish between tangents to the spacetime M and tangents to an associated flat affine fiber space, X. X is a (pseudo-) Euclidean space (a Minkowski space) with metric g and no origin, so you cannot add two points in X or multiply a point in X by a scalar. The affine connection tells us how to parallel translate points in X and tangents to X along curves in M, not how to parallel translate tangents to M. The translational part of the affine connection acts like an (inverse) frame field that enables us to identify tangents to M with tangents to X, and pulls back the metric g on X to a metric on M. While the distinction between tangents to M and tangents to X at first may seem artificial, the equations of Einstein-Cartan theory become conceptually and computationally simpler when conserved currents (like momentum and spin) are represented by tangents to X, which are parallel translated by the connection, and directions in M (and flux boxes through which conserved currents flow) are represented by tangents to M, which never need to be parallel translated along a curve in M. In this article, we use Roman indices i,j,k,... to denote tangent vectors to M and Roman indices a,b,c,... to denote tangents to the fiber space X. For example the momentum tensor

$$P_a^k$$

represents the flux normal to the spacetime k-direction of momentum in the a-direction, and the spin tensor

$$\sigma_{ab}{}^{k}$$

represents the flux normal to the spacetime k-direction of spin in the a,b plane.

(Advanced point: In order to accommodate spinor fields, all of the constructions of Riemannian and Riemann-Cartan geometry can be generalized from orthogonal groups, principal orthogonal frame bundles and associated tangent bundles to spin groups, principal spin bundles and associated spinor bundles. A spacetime manifold admits a spin bundle over its principal frame bundle only if the second Stiefel-Whitney class of M is zero. The Riemann tensor is the curvature form for (generalized to include boosts) rotations (i.e. the spin(p,q) part) while torsion is the curvature form for translations (R_4.)

A geometric interpretation of affine torsion comes from continuum mechanics of solid materials. Affine torsion is the continuum approximation to the distribution of dislocations that are studied in metallurgy and crystallography. The simplest kinds of dislocations in real crystals are

- edge dislocations (formed by adding an extra half-plane of atoms to a perfect crystal, so you get a defect in the regular crystal structure along the line where the extra half-plane ends), and
- screw dislocations (formed by inserting a "parking garage ramp" that extends to the edges of the garage into an otherwise perfectly layered structure).

We can think of a Riemann-Cartan geometry as uniquely determined by the lengths and angles of vectors and the density of dislocations in the affine structure of the space.

General relativity set the affine torsion to zero, because it did not appear necessary to provide a model of gravitation (with a consistent set of equations that led to a well-defined initial value problem).

Derivation of field equations of Einstein-Cartan theory

General relativity and Einstein-Cartan theory both use the scalar curvature as Lagrangian. General relativity obtains its field equations by varying the Einstein-Hilbert action (integral of the Lagrangian over spacetime) with respect to the metric tensor. The result is the famous Einstein equations:

$$R_{ab} - \frac{1}{2} R g_{ab} = \frac{8\pi G}{c^4} P_{ab}$$

where

- R_{ab} are the Ricci tensor components (a contraction of the full Riemann curvature tensor that has four indices).
- g_{ab} are the (symmetric nondegenerate) metric tensor components.
- R is the scalar curvature (Ricci scalar).
- P_{ab} are the energy-momentum tensor components. (We reserve the symbol T, which is the usual symbol for the energy-momentum tensor in general relativity, for the affine torsion.)
- G is the Newtonian gravitational constant.
- c is the speed of light.

The contracted second Bianchi identity of Riemannian geometry becomes, in general relativity,

$$divP = P^{ab};b = 0$$

which makes conservation of energy and momentum equivalent to an identity of Riemannian geometry.

A basic question in formulating Einstein-Cartan theory is which variables in the action to vary to get the field equations. You can vary the metric tensor g_{ij} and the torsion tensor $T_{ij}^{\ \ k}$. However, this makes the equations of Einstein-Cartan theory messier than necessary and disguises the geometric content of the theory. The key insight is to let the symmetry group of Einstein-Cartan theory be the inhomogeneous rotation group (which includes translations in space and time), that is, the analogue of the Euclidean group. (The inhomogeneous rotational symmetry is broken by the fact that the zero point in each tangent fiber is still a preferred point, as in ordinary Riemannian geometry based on the homogeneous rotation group.) We vary the action with respect to the affine connection coefficients associated with translational and rotational symmetries. (A similar approach in general relativity is called *Palatini variation*, in which the action is varied with respect to the rotational connection coefficients instead of the metric; general relativity has no translational connection coefficients.)

The resulting field equations of Einstein-Cartan theory are:

$$R_a^{\ k} - \frac{1}{2} g_a^{\ k} R = \frac{8\pi G}{c^{\perp}} P_a^{\ k}$$

$$S_{ab}{}^{k} = \frac{8\pi G}{c^4}\sigma_{ab}{}^{k}$$

where

- $\sigma_{ab}{}^{k}$ is the spin tensor of all matter and radiation
- $S_{ab}{}^{k} = T_{ab}{}^{k} + g_a{}^{k}T_m{}^{m} — g_a{}^{k}T_m$ is the modified torsion tensor
- $T_{ab}{}^{k}$ is the affine torsion tensor.

The first equation is the same as in general relativity, except that the affine torsion is included in all the curvature terms, so p_{aj} need not be symmetric.

The contracted second Bianchi identity of Riemann-Cartan geometry becomes, in Einstein-Cartan theory,

- div(P) = some very small terms that are products of curvature and torsion,
- div(Spin) = — antisymmetric part of p_{aj}.

The conservation of momentum is altered by products of gravitational field strength and spin density. These terms are exceedingly small under normal conditions, and they seem reasonable in that the gravitational field itself carries energy. The second equation is conservation of angular momentum, in a form that accommodates spin-orbit coupling.

Geometric insights from Einstein-Cartan theory

First geometric insight

Spin (intrinsic angular momentum) consists of a (continuous or discrete) distribution of dislocations in the fabric of spacetime. For ordinary fermions (particles with half-integer spin such as protons, neutrons and electrons), these are screw dislocations (parking garage ramps) with timelike direction of the screw. That is, for a particle with spin in the +*Z* direction, traversing a space-like loop in the *X*-*y* plane around the particle parallel translates you into the past or the future by a small amount.

Second geometric insight

It has long been known that the spin angular momentum tensor

$$\sigma_{ab}{}^{k}$$

is the Noether current of rotational symmetry of spacetime, and the momentum tensor

$$P_a{}^{k}$$

is the Noether current of translational symmetry. (The Noether theorem states that, for every symmetry of a physical system, there is a corresponding conserved current derived by performing the symmetry transformation on the Lagrangian.) Einstein-Cartan theory provides a clean derivation of momentum as the Noether current of translational symmetry. General relativity without translational connection coefficients (which would introduce affine torsion into the theory) does not provide a clean derivation of the momentum as the Noether current of translational symmetry.

Third geometric insight

Expressing Einstein-Cartan theory in the simplest form requires distinguishing two kinds of tensor indices:

1. indices that represent conserved currents like momentum and spin. Geometrically, these indices represent directions in the idealized Minkowski "fiber space" at each point of spacetime. (Notation used here: *a, b, c...*)
2. indices that represent spacetime boxes through which fluxes of the currents are measured. Geometrically, these indices represent tangents to the spacetime base manifold that describe boxes through which the fluxes of conserved currents are measured. (Notation used here: *i, j, k ...*)

This is similar to other gauge theories, like electromagnetism and Yang-Mills theory, where we would never confuse spacetime indices that represent flux boxes with the fiber indices that represent the conserved currents.

All the derivative indices in Einstein-Cartan theory are spacetime (base space) indices. Furthermore, the derivatives are all 'exterior derivatives,' which measure fluxes of currents through spacetime boxes (or divergences, which are Hodge duals of exterior derivatives). All the indices that are antisymmetrized with derivative indices in exterior derivatives (or the indices with which the derivative indices are contracted in divergences) are also spacetime indices. All these indices are part of the calculus of flux boxes in spacetime, and do not represent the conserved currents themselves.

The statement that all derivatives are covariant exterior derivatives boils down to the fact that the affine connection is a law of parallel translation for points in the affine fiber space X, and not a law of parallel translation for tangent vectors to the base manifold M. In fact, we don't have ANY connection on the tangent bundle TM of M. The Levi-Civita metric connection that is often highlighted in treatments of general relativity is merely a computational convenience for writing exterior derivatives and divergences involving spacetime indices, which has nothing to do with parallel translation.

For example, in the field equations of Einstein-Cartan theory stated above, we should interpret the indices a, b as fiber indices and the indices i,j as base space indices. The momentum tensor

$$P_a^{\ k}$$

describes the flux of a-momentum through a flux box normal to the k-direction in spacetime, and the spin tensor Spina,bk describes the flux of angular momentum in the a × b plane through a flux box normal to the k-direction in spacetime.

NB: Before the distinction between these types of indices became clear, researchers would vary the action with respect to the metric to get what they called the "momentum tensor" (the 'wrong' one) and also sometimes vary with respect to the translational connection coefficients and get a different momentum tensor (the 'right' one) and they did not know which one was the real momentum tensor. The equations of the theory had many unnecessary terms because they did not distinguish between the base space and fiber space tensor indices.)

Fourth geometric insight

Einstein-Cartan theory is about defects in the affine (Euclidean-like but curved) structure of spacetime; it is not a metric theory of gravitation.

We have seen above that the affine torsion is a continuum model of dislocation density. The full rotational (or Riemannian) curvature tensor

$$R_{klb}{}^{a}$$

also has an interpretation as a density of defects in continuum mechanics. It is the continuum model of a density of "disclination defects." A disclination results when you make a cut into a continuum (imagine making a radial cut from the edge to the center of a disk of rubber) and insert (or excise) an angular wedge of material, so that the sum of the angles surrounding the endpoint of the cut is more than (or less than) 2p radians. (Indeed, this procedure can convert a flat disk into a bowl: make many small radial cuts from the edge with varying lengths part-way to the center, excise wedges of material of the appropriate angular width, and sew up the cuts.)

The central role of affine defects explains why the clean way to do Einstein-Cartan theory is to vary the translational and rotational connection coefficients (not the metric) and to distinguish between the base space and fiber indices. The connection coefficients are keeping track of the dislocation and disclination defects in the affine structure of spacetime. It is as if spacetime were composed of many microcrystals of perfectly flat Minkowski space, and these perfect micro-pieces are fit together with defects like dislocations and disclinations.

The central role of the translational and rotational connection coefficients as field variables is recognized in modern efforts to quantize general relativity under the name "Ashtekar variables." The Ashtekar variables are essentially the translational and rotational connection coefficients, suitably worked into a Hamiltonian formulation of general relativity.

General relativity plus matter with spin implies Einstein-Cartan theory

For decades, it was thought that Einstein-Cartan theory is based on an independent assumption to include affine torsion. Since the effect of torsion is too small to measure empirically so far, Einstein-Cartan theory was considered one of many speculative (and largely ignored) extensions of general relativity.

Binary pulsar PSR J0737-3039A/B may be a test of relativistic spin-orbit coupling (Breton, *et al.*, 2008).

It has been shown that general relativity plus a fluid of many tiny rotating black holes generate affine torsion and essentially the equations of Einstein-Cartan theory (Petti, 1986). If we introduce a classical spin fluid with spin-orbit coupling, torsion is necessary to describe the spin-orbit coupling. (Example of a classical spin fluid: Approximate a distribution of galaxies with correlated rotations as a classical fluid with spin. In this approximation, the rotational angular momentum of the galaxies becomes intrinsic angular momentum, that is, spin.) The "proof" uses a standard Kerr-Newman rotating black hole solution of general relativity. It computes the non-Zero time-like translation that occurs when you parallel-translate an affine frame (keeping track of translation as well as rotation) around an equatorial loop near the black hole. The main conclusion (that general relativity plus spin-orbit coupling implies nonzero torsion and Einstein-Cartan theory) can be derived from classical physics and classical differential geometry without recourse to quantum mechanical spin or spinor fields. The word "proof" appears in quotes because, while it is intuitively compelling that this implies Einstein-Cartan theory, the rigorous mathematical proof of convergence to the equations of Einstein-Cartan theory has not been done.

Adamowicz showed that general relativity plus a linearized classical model of matter with spin yields the same linearized equations for the time-time and space-space components of the metric as linearized Einstein-Cartan theory (Adamowicz 1975). Adamowicz does not treat the time-space components of the metric, the spin-torsion field equation, spin-orbit coupling and the non-symmetric momentum tensor, the geometry of torsion, or quantum mechanical spin. He says, "It is possible a priori to solve this problem [of dust with intrinsic angular momentum] exactly in the formalism of general relativity but in the general situation we have no practical approach because of mathematical difficulties." Adamowicz's conclusion is at best incomplete: it is not possible to solve the full problem exactly in general relativity, including spin-orbit coupling, without adopting the larger framework of EC theory.

A GR theory with only scalar and Maxwell (i.e. massless vector) fields need not have a nonzero torsion. If we introduce spinorial fields, then we also have to introduce a spin connection. The Euler-Lagrange equation for pure GR or GR with scalar and Maxwell fields does not involve the connection except in the Einstein-Hilbert action and states that the theory is torsionless. However, once we introduce spinor fields which have to couple to the spin connection, the Euler-Lagrange equation now equates the torsion with the result of varying the matter action with the spin connection. In fact, the standard definition of the stress-energy tensor as the result of varying the matter action with respect to the metric tensor can no longer apply because spinors couple to vierbeins and the spin connection instead. Instead, we now have to define the stress-energy tensor has the result of varying the matter action with respect to the vierbein. This stress-energy tensor is now no longer symmetric and if we define the spin tensor as the result of varying the matter action with respect to the spin connection, we find that the antisymmetric part of the stress-energy tensor is equal to the divergence of the spin tensor.

Einstein-Podolsky-Rosen Paradox or EPR Paradox

In quantum mechanics, the EPR paradox (or Einstein-Podolsky-Rosen paradox) is a thought experiment which challenged long-held ideas about the relation between the observed values of physical quantities and the values that can be accounted for by a physical theory. Einstein, Podolsky, and Rosen introduced the thought experiment in a 1935 paper to argue that quantum mechanics is not a complete physical theory.

According to its authors the EPR experiment yields a dichotomy. Either,

1. The result of a measurement performed on one part A of a quantum system has a non-local effect on the physical reality of another distant part B, in the sense that quantum mechanics can predict outcomes of some measurements carried out at B; or...
2. Quantum mechanics is incomplete in the sense that some element of physical reality corresponding to B

cannot be accounted for by quantum mechanics (that is, some extra variable is needed to account for it).

As shown later by Bell, one cannot introduce the notion of "elements of reality" without affecting the predictions of the theory. That is, one cannot complete quantum mechanics with these "elements", because this automatically leads to some logical contradictions.

Einstein never accepted quantum mechanics as a "real" and complete theory, struggling to the end of his life for an interpretation that could comply with relativity without complying with the Heisenberg Uncertainty Principle. As he once said: "God does not play dice", skeptically referring to the Copenhagen Interpretation of quantum mechanics which says there exists no objective physical reality other than that which is revealed through measurement and observation.

The EPR paradox is a paradox in the following sense: if one adds to quantum mechanics some seemingly reasonable (but actually wrong, or questionable as a whole) conditions — like local realism (not to be confused with philosophical realism), counterfactual definiteness, and incompleteness — then one obtains a contradiction. However, quantum mechanics by itself does not appear to be internally inconsistent, nor — as it turns out — does it contradict relativity. As a result of further theoretical and experimental developments since the original EPR paper, most physicists today regard the EPR paradox as an illustration of how quantum mechanics violates classical intuitions.

Quantum mechanics and its interpretation

Since the early twentieth century, quantum theory has proved to be very successful, describing accurately the physical reality of the mesoscopic and microscopic world. This fact has been made clear through multiple, repeatable or falsifiable physical experiments.

Quantum mechanics was developed with the aim of describing atoms and explaining the observed spectral lines in a measurement apparatus. Though disputed, it has never been seriously challenged. Philosophical interpretations of quantum phenomena, however, are another story: the question of how to interpret the mathematical formulation of quantum mechanics has given rise to a variety of different answers from people of different philosophical backgrounds.

Quantum theory and quantum mechanics do not account for single measurement outcomes in a deterministic way. According to an accepted interpretation of quantum mechanics known as the Copenhagen interpretation, a measurement causes an instantaneous collapse of the wave function describing the quantum system into an eigenstate of the observable that was measured.

The most prominent opponent of the Copenhagen interpretation was Albert Einstein. Einstein did not believe in the idea of genuine randomness in nature, the main argument in the Copenhagen interpretation. In his view, quantum mechanics is incomplete and suggests that there had to be 'hidden' variables responsible for random measurement results.

The famous paper *"Can Quantum-Mechanical Description of Physical Reality Be Considered Complete?"*, authored by Einstein, Podolsky and Rosen in 1935, condensed the philosophical discussion into a physical argument. They claim that given a specific experiment, in which the outcome of a measurement could be known before the measurement takes place, there must exist something in the real world, an "element of reality", which determines the measurement outcome. They postulate that these elements of reality are local, in the sense that each belongs to a certain point in spacetime. Each element may only be influenced by events which are located in the backward light cone of its point in spacetime. These claims are founded on assumptions about nature which constitute what is now known as local realism.

Though the EPR paper has often been taken as an exact expression of Einstein's views, it was primarily authored by Podolsky, based on discussions at the Institute for Advanced Study with Einstein and Rosen. Einstein later expressed to Erwin Schrödinger that "It did not come out as well as I had originally wanted; rather, the essential thing was, so to speak, smothered by the formalism."

Description of the paradox

The EPR paradox draws on a phenomenon predicted by quantum mechanics, known as quantum entanglement, to show that measurements performed on spatially separated parts of a quantum system can apparently have an instantaneous influence on one another.

This effect is now known as "nonlocal behaviour" (or colloquially as "quantum weirdness" or "spooky action at a distance").

Simple version

Before delving into the complicated logic that leads to the 'paradox', it is perhaps worth mentioning the simple version of the argument, as described by Greene and others, which Einstein used to show that 'hidden variables' must exist.

A positron and an electron are emitted from a source, by pion decay, so that their spins are opposite; one particle's spin about any axis is the negative of the other's. Also, due to uncertainty, making a measurement of a particle's spin about one axis disturbs the particle so you now can't measure its spin about any other axis.

Now say you measure the electron's spin about the X-axis. This automatically tells you the positron's spin about the X-axis. Since you've done the measurement *without disturbing the positron in any way,* it can't be that the positron "only came to have that state when you measured it", because you didn't measure it! It must have had that spin *all along.* Also you can now measure the positron's spin about the *y*-axis. So it follows that the positron has had a definite spin about two axes — much more information than the positron is capable of holding, and a "hidden variable" according to EPR.

Measurements on an entangled state

We have a source that emits electron-positron pairs, with the electron sent to destination A, where there is an observer named Alice, and the positron sent to destination *B,* where there is an observer named Bob. According to quantum mechanics, we can arrange our source so that each emitted pair occupies a quantum state called a spin singlet. This can be viewed as a quantum superposition of two states, which we call state I and state II. In state I, the electron has spin pointing upward along the *Z*-axis (+*Z*) and the positron has spin pointing downward along the *Z*-axis (-*Z*). In state II, the electron has spin -*Z* and the positron has spin +*Z*. Therefore, it is impossible to associate either particle in the spin singlet with a state of definite spin. The particles are thus said to be entangled.

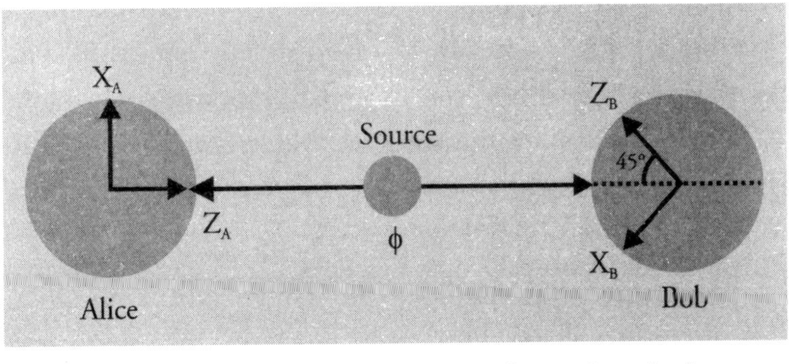

The EPR thought experiment, performed with electron-positron pairs. A source (center) sends particles toward two observers, electrons to Alice (left) and positrons to Bob (right), who can perform spin measurements.

Alice now measures the spin along the *Z*-axis. She can obtain one of two possible outcomes: +*Z* or -*Z*. Suppose she gets +*Z*. According to quantum mechanics, the quantum state of the system collapses into state I. (Different interpretations of quantum mechanics have different ways of saying this, but the basic result is the same.) The quantum state determines the probable outcomes of any measurement performed on the system. In this case, if Bob subsequently measures spin along the *Z*-axis, he will obtain -*Z* with 100% probability. Similarly, if Alice gets -*Z*, Bob will get +*Z*.

There is, of course, nothing special about our choice of the *Z*-axis. For instance, suppose that Alice and Bob now decide to measure spin along the *X*-axis, according to quantum mechanics, the spin singlet state may equally well be expressed as a superposition of spin states pointing in the x direction. We'll call these states Ia and IIa. In state Ia, Alice's electron has spin +*X* and Bob's positron has spin -*X*. In state IIa, Alice's electron has spin -X and Bob's positron has spin +*X*. Therefore, if Alice measures +*X*, the system collapses into Ia, and Bob will get -*X*. If Alice measures -*X*, the system collapses into IIa, and Bob will get +*X*.

In quantum mechanics, the *X*-spin and *Z*-spin are "incompatible observables", which means that there is a Heisenberg uncertainty principle operating between them: a quantum state cannot possess a definite value for both variables. Suppose Alice measures the *Z*-spin and obtains +*Z*, so that the quantum state collapses into state I. Now, instead of measuring the *Z*-spin as well, Bob measures the *X*-spin. According to quantum mechanics, when the system is in state I, Bob's *X*-spin measurement will have a 50% probability of producing +*X* and a 50% probability of -*X*. Furthermore, it is fundamentally impossible to predict which outcome will appear until Bob actually performs the measurement.

Here is the crux of the matter. You might imagine that, when Bob measures the *X*-spin of his positron, he would get an answer with absolute certainty, since prior to this he hasn't disturbed his particle at all. But, as described above, Bob's positron has a 50% probability of producing +*X* and a 50% probability of -*X*-random behaviour, not certain. Bob's positron knows that Alice's electron has been measured, and its *Z*-spin detected, and hence B's *Z*-spin calculated, so its *X*-spin is 'out of bounds'.

Put another way, how does Bob's positron know, at the same time, which way to point if Alice decides (based on information unavailable to Bob) to measure x (i.e. be the opposite of Alice's electron's spin about the *X*-axis) and *also* how to point if Alice measures *z* (i.e. behave randomly), since it is only supposed to know one thing at a time? Using the usual Copenhagen interpretation rules that say the wave function "collapses" at the time of measurement, there must be action at a distance (entanglement) or the positron must know more than it is supposed to (hidden variables).

In case the explanation above is confusing, here is the paradox summed up:

An electron-positron pair is emitted, the particles shoot off and are measured later. Whatever axis their spins are measured along, they are always found to be opposite. This can only be explained if the particles are linked in some way. Either they were created with a definite (opposite) spin about every axis—a "hidden variable" argument—or they are *linked* so that one electron knows what axis the other is having its spin measured along, and becomes its opposite about that one axis—an "entanglement" argument. Moreover, if the two particles have their spins measured about *different* axes, once the electron's spin has been measured about the *X*-axis (and the positron's spin about the *X*-axis deduced), the positron's spin about the y-axis will no longer be certain, as if it knows that the measurement has taken place. Either that or it has a definite spin already, which gives it a spin about a second axis—a hidden variable.

Incidentally, although we have used spin as an example, many types of physical quantities—what quantum mechanics refers to as "observables"-can be used to produce quantum entanglement. The original EPR paper used momentum for the observable. Experimental realizations of the EPR scenario often use photon polarization, because polarized photons are easy to prepare and measure.

Locality in the EPR experiment

The principle of locality states that physical processes occurring at one place should have no immediate effect on the elements of reality at another location. At first sight, this appears to be a reasonable assumption to make, as it seems to be a consequence of special relativity, which states that information can never be transmitted faster than the speed of light without violating causality. It is generally believed that any theory which violates causality would also be internally inconsistent, and thus deeply unsatisfactory.

It turns out that the usual rules for combining quantum mechanical and classical descriptions violate the principle of locality without violating causality. Causality is preserved because there is no way for Alice to transmit messages (i.e. information) to Bob by manipulating her measurement axis. Whichever axis she uses, she has a 50% probability of obtaining "+" and 50% probability of obtaining "-", completely at random; according to quantum mechanics, it is fundamentally impossible for her to influence what result she gets. Furthermore, Bob is only able to perform his measurement once: there is a fundamental property of quantum mechanics, known as the "no cloning theorem", which makes it impossible for him to make a million copies of the electron he receives, perform a spin measurement on each, and look at the statistical distribution of the results. Therefore, in the one measurement he is allowed to make, there is a 50% probability of getting "+" and 50% of getting "–", regardless of whether or not his axis is aligned with Alice's.

However, the principle of locality appeals powerfully to physical intuition, and Einstein, Podolsky and Rosen were unwilling to abandon it. Einstein derided the quantum mechanical predictions as "spooky action at a distance". The conclusion they drew was that quantum mechanics is not a complete theory.

In recent years, however, doubt has been cast on EPR's conclusion due to developments in understanding locality and especially quantum decoherence. The word locality has several different meanings in physics. For example, in quantum field theory "locality" means that quantum fields at different points of space do not interact with one another. However, quantum field theories that are "local" in this sense *appear* to violate the principle of locality as defined by EPR, but they nevertheless do not violate locality in a more general sense. Wavefunction collapse can be viewed as an epiphenomenon of quantum decoherence, which in turn is nothing more than an effect of the underlying local time evolution of the wavefunction of a system and *all* of its environment. Since the *underlying* behaviour doesn't violate local causality, it follows that neither does the additional effect of wavefunction collapse, whether real *or* apparent. Therefore, as outlined in the example above, neither the EPR experiment nor any quantum experiment demonstrates that faster-than-light signaling is possible.

Resolving the paradox

Hidden variables

There are several ways to resolve the EPR paradox. The one suggested by EPR is that quantum mechanics, despite its success in a wide variety of experimental scenarios, is actually an incomplete theory. In other words, there is some yet undiscovered theory of nature to which quantum mechanics acts as a kind of statistical approximation (albeit an exceedingly successful one). Unlike quantum mechanics, the more complete theory contains variables corresponding to all the "elements of reality". There must be some unknown mechanism acting on these variables to give rise to the observed effects of "non-commuting quantum observables", i.e. the Heisenberg uncertainty principle. Such a theory is called a hidden variable theory.

To illustrate this idea, we can formulate a very simple hidden variable theory for the above thought experiment. One supposes that the quantum spin-singlet states emitted by the source are actually approximate descriptions for "true" physical states possessing definite values for the *Z*-spin and *X*-spin. In these "true" states, the electron going to Bob always has spin values opposite to the electron going to Alice, but the values are otherwise completely random. For example, the first pair emitted by the source might be "(+*Z*, -*X*) to Alice and (-*Z*, +*X*) to Bob", the next pair "(-*Z*, -*X*) to Alice and (+*Z*, +*X*) to Bob", and so forth. Therefore, if Bob's measurement axis is aligned with Alice's, he will necessarily get the opposite of whatever Alice gets; otherwise, he will get "+" and "-" with equal probability.

Assuming we restrict our measurements to the Z and X axes, such a hidden variable theory is experimentally indistinguishable from quantum mechanics. In reality, of course, there is an (uncountably) infinite number of axes along which Alice and Bob can perform their measurements, so there has to be an infinite number of independent hidden variables. However, this is not a serious problem; we have formulated a very simplistic hidden variable theory, and a more sophisticated theory might be able to patch it up. It turns out that there is a much more serious challenge to the idea of hidden variables.

Bell's inequality

In 1964, John Bell showed that the predictions of quantum mechanics in the EPR thought experiment are significantly different from the predictions of a very broad class of hidden variable theories (the local hidden variable theories). Roughly speaking, quantum mechanics predicts much stronger statistical correlations between the measurement results performed on different axes than the hidden variable theories. These differences, expressed using inequality relations known as "Bell's inequalities", are in principle experimentally detectable. Later work by Eberhard showed that the key properties of local hidden variable theories that lead to Bell's inequalities are locality and counter-factual definiteness. Any theory in which these principles hold produces the inequalities. A. Fine subsequently showed that any theory satisfying the inequalities can be modeled by a local hidden variable theory.

After the publication of Bell's paper, a variety of experiments were devised to test Bell's inequalities. (As mentioned above, these experiments generally rely on photon polarization measurements.) All the experiments conducted to date have found behaviour in line with the predictions of standard quantum mechanics.

However, Bell's theorem does not apply to all possible philosophically realist theories, although a common misconception is that quantum mechanics is inconsistent with all notions of philosophical realism. Realist interpretations of quantum mechanics are possible, although as discussed above, such interpretations must reject either locality or counter-factual definiteness. Mainstream physics prefers to keep locality while still maintaining a notion of realism that nevertheless rejects counter-factual definiteness. Examples of such mainstream realist interpretations are the consistent histories interpretation and the transactional interpretation. Fine's work showed that taking locality as a given there exist scenarios in which two statistical variables are correlated in a manner inconsistent with counter-factual definiteness and that such scenarios are no more mysterious than any other despite the inconsistency with counter-factual definiteness seeming 'counter-intuitive'. Violation of locality however is difficult to reconcile with special relativity and is thought to be incompatible with the principle of causality. On the other hand the Bohm interpretation of quantum mechanics instead keeps counter-factual definiteness while introducing a conjectured non-local mechanism called the 'quantum potential'. Some workers in the field have also attempted to formulate hidden variable theories that exploit loopholes in actual experiments, such as the assumptions made in interpreting experimental data although no such theory has been produced that can reproduce all the results of quantum mechanics.

There are also individual EPR-like experiments that have no local hidden variables explanation. Examples have been suggested by David Bohm and by Lucien Hardy.

Einstein's hope for a purely algebraic theory

The Bohm interpretation of quantum mechanics hypothesizes that the state of the universe evolves smoothly through time with no collapsing of quantum wavefunctions. One problem for the Copenhagen interpretation is to precisely define wavefunction collapse. Einstein maintained that quantum mechanics is physically incomplete and logically unsatisfactory. In "The Meaning of Relativity," Einstein wrote, "One can give good reasons why reality cannot at all be represented by a continuous field. From the quantum phenomena it appears to follow with certainty that a finite system of finite energy can be completely described by a finite set of numbers (quantum numbers). This does not seem to be in accordance with a continuum theory and must lead to an attempt to find a purely algebraic theory for the representation of reality. But nobody knows how to find the basis for such a theory." If time, space, and energy are secondary features derived from a substrate below the Planck scale, then Einstein's hypothetical algebraic system might resolve the EPR paradox (although Bell's theorem would still be valid). Edward Fredkin in the Fredkin Finite Nature Hypothesis has suggested an informational basis for Einstein's hypothetical algebraic system. If physical reality is totally finite, then the Copenhagen interpretation might be an approximation to an information processing system below the Planck scale.

"Acceptable theories", and the experiment

According to the present view of the situation, quantum mechanics simply contradicts Einstein's philosophical postulate that any acceptable physical theory should fulfill "local realism".

In the EPR paper (1935) the authors realized that quantum mechanics was non-acceptable in the sense of their above-mentioned assumptions, and Einstein thought erroneously that it could simply be augmented by 'hidden variables', without any further change, to get an acceptable theory. He pursued these ideas until the end of his life (1955), over twenty years.

In contrast, John Bell, in his 1964 paper, showed "once and for all" that quantum mechanics and Einstein's assumptions lead to different results, different by a factor of for certain correlations. So the issue of "acceptability", up to this time mainly concerning theory (*even philosophy*), finally became *experimentally* decidable.

There are many Bell test experiments hitherto, e.g. those of Alain Aspect and others. They all show that pure *quantum mechanics,* and *not* Einstein's "local realism", is acceptable. Thus, according to Karl Popper these experiments *falsify* Einstein's philosophical assumptions, especially the ideas on "hidden variables", whereas quantum mechanics itself remains a good candidate for a theory, which is acceptable in a wider context.

Implications for quantum mechanics

Most physicists today believe that quantum mechanics is correct, and that the EPR paradox is a "paradox" only because classical intuitions do not correspond to physical reality. How EPR is interpreted regarding locality depends on the interpretation of quantum mechanics one uses. In the Copenhagen interpretation, it is usually understood that instantaneous wavefunction collapse does occur. However, the view that there is no causal instantaneous effect has also been proposed within the Copenhagen interpretation: in this alternate view, measurement affects our ability to define (and measure) quantities in the physical system, not the system itself. In the many-worlds interpretation, a kind of locality is preserved, since the effects of irreversible operations such as measurement arise from the relativization of a global state to a subsystem such as that of an observer.

The EPR paradox has deepened our understanding of quantum mechanics by exposing the fundamentally non-classical characteristics of the measurement process. Prior to the publication of the EPR paper, a measurement was often visualized as a physical disturbance inflicted directly upon the measured system. For instance, when measuring the position of an electron, one imagines shining a light on it, thus disturbing the electron and producing the quantum mechanical uncertainties in its position. Such explanations, which are still encountered in popular expositions of quantum mechanics, are debunked by the EPR paradox, which shows that a "measurement" can be performed on a particle without disturbing it directly, by performing a measurement on a distant entangled particle.

Technologies relying on quantum entanglement are now being developed. In quantum cryptography, entangled particles are used to transmit signals that cannot be eavesdropped upon without leaving a trace. In quantum computation, entangled quantum states are used to perform computations in parallel, which may allow certain calculations to be performed much more quickly than they ever could be with classical computers.

Equations of Motion

The theory of general relativity has two fundamental laws — the Einstein equations which describe how space curves, and the geodesic equation which describes how particles move.

Since the equations of general relativity are non-linear, a lump of energy made out of pure gravitational fields, like a black hole, would move on a trajectory which is determined by the Einstein equations themselves, not by a new law.

So Einstein proposed that the path of a singular solution, like a black hole, would be determined to be a geodesic from general relativity itself.

This was established by Einstein, Infeld and Hoffmann for pointlike objects without angular momentum, and by Roy Kerr for spinning objects.

Einstein-Infeld-Hoffmann equation

The Einstein-Infeld-Hofmann equation, jointly derived by Albert Einstein, Leopold Infeld and Banesh Hoffmann, is a differential equation of motion describing the approximate dynamics of a system of point-like masses due to their mutual gravitational interactions, including general relativistic effects. It uses a first order Post-Newtonian expansion and thus is valid in the limit where the velocities of the bodies are small compared to the speed of light and where the gravitational fields affecting them are correspondingly weak.

Given a system of N bodies, labelled by indices A = 1, ..., N, the barycentric acceleration vector of body A is given by:

$$
\begin{aligned}
\vec{a}_A &= \sum_{B \neq A} \frac{G m_B \vec{n}_{BA}}{r_{AB}^2} \\
&+ \frac{1}{c^2} \sum_{B \neq A} \frac{G m_B \vec{n}_{BA}}{r_{AB}^2} \left[v_A^2 + 2v_B^2 - 4(\vec{v}_A \cdot \vec{v}_B) - \frac{3}{2}(\vec{n}_{AB} \cdot \vec{v}_B)^2 \right. \\
&\quad \left. -4 \sum_{C \neq A} \frac{G m_C}{r_{AC}} - \sum_{C \neq B} \frac{G m_C}{r_{BC}} + \frac{1}{2}((\vec{x}_B - \vec{x}_A) \cdot \vec{a}_B) \right] \\
&+ \frac{1}{c^2} \sum_{B \neq A} \frac{G m_B}{r_{AB}^2} \left[\vec{n}_{AB} \cdot (4\vec{v}_A - 3\vec{v}_B) \right] (\vec{v}_A - \vec{v}_B) \\
&+ \frac{7}{2c^2} \sum_{B \neq A} \frac{G m_B \vec{a}_B}{r_{AB}}
\end{aligned}
$$

$\vec{x}_A$ is the barycentric position vector of body A

A$\vec{v}_A = d\vec{x}_A / dt$ is the barycentric velocity vector of body A

$\vec{a}_A = d^2\vec{x}_A / dt^2$ is the barycentric acceleration vector of body A

$r_{AB} = |\vec{x}_A - \vec{x}_B|$ is the coordinate distance between bodies A and B

$\vec{n}_{AB} = (\vec{x}_A - \vec{x}_B)/r_{AB}$ is the unit vector pointing from body B to body A

Am_A is the mass of body A.

c is the speed of light

G is the gravitational constant.

The coordinates used here are harmonic. The first term on the right hand side is the Newtonian gravitational acceleration at A; in the limit as c? 8, one recovers Newton's law of motion.

The acceleration of a particular body depends on the accelerations of all the other bodies. Since the quantity on the left hand side also appears in the right hand side, this system of equations must be solved iteratively. In practice, using the Newtonian acceleration instead of the true acceleration provides sufficient accuracy.

Einstein's Mistakes

In addition to his well-accepted results, some of Einstein's papers contain mistakes:

- **1905:** In the original German version of the special relativity paper, and in some English translations, Einstein gives a wrong expression for the transverse mass of a fast moving particle. The transverse mass is the antiquated name for the ratio of the 3-force to the 3-acceleration when the force is perpendicular to the velocity. Einstein gives this ratio as $m\left(1-v^2/c^2\right)$, while the actual value is $m/\sqrt{1-v^2/c^2}$ (corrected by Max Planck).

- 1905: In his PhD dissertation, the friction in dilute solutions has a miscalculated numerical prefactor, which makes the estimate of Avogadro's number off by a factor of 3. The mistake is corrected by Einstein in a later publication.

- 1905: An expository paper explaining how airplanes fly includes an example which is incorrect. There is a wing which he claims will generate lift. This wing is flat on the bottom, and flat on the top, with a small bump at the center. It is designed to generate lift by Bernoulli's principle, and Einstein claims that it will. Simple action reaction considerations, though, show that the wing will not generate lift, at least if it is long enough.

- 1911: Einstein predicted how much the sun's gravity would deflect nearby starlight, but used an approximation which gives an answer which is half as big as the correct one.
- 1913: Einstein started writing papers based on his belief that the hole argument made general covariance impossible in a theory of gravity.
- 1922: Einstein published a qualitative theory of superconductivity based on the vague idea of electrons shared in orbits. This paper predated modern quantum mechanics, and is well understood to be completely wrong. The correct BCS theory of low temperature superconductivity was only worked out in 1957, thirty years after the establishing of modern quantum mechanics.
- 1937: Einstein believed that the focusing properties of geodesics in general relativity would lead to an instability which causes plane gravitational waves to collapse in on themselves. While this is true to a certain extent in some limits, because gravitational instabilities can lead to a concentration of energy density into black holes, for plane waves of the type Einstein and Rosen considered in their paper, the

instabilities are under control. Einstein retracted this position a short time later, but until his death, his collaborator Nathan Rosen maintained that gravitational waves are unstable.

- 1939: Einstein denied several times that black holes could form, the last time in print. He published a paper that argues that a star collapsing would spin faster and faster, spinning at the speed of light with infinite energy well before the point where it is about to collapse into a black hole. This paper received no citations, and the conclusions are well understood to be wrong. Einstein's argument itself is inconclusive, since he only shows that stable spinning objects have to spin faster and faster to stay stable before the point where they collapse. But it is well understood today (and was understood well by some even then) that collapse cannot happen through stationary states the way Einstein imagined.

In addition to these well established mistakes, there are other arguments whose deduction is considered correct, but whose interpretation or philosophical conclusion is considered to have been incorrect:

- In the Bohr-Einstein debates and the papers following this, Einstein tries to poke holes in the uncertainty principle, ingeniously, but unsuccessfully.

- In the EPR paper, Einstein concludes that quantum mechanics must be replaced by local hidden variables. The measured violations of Bell's inequality show that hidden variables, if they exist, must be nonlocal.

Einstein himself considered the use of the "fudge factor" lambda in his 1917 paper founding cosmology as a "blunder". The theory of general relativity predicted an expanding or contracting universe, but Einstein wanted a universe which is an unchanging three dimensional sphere, like the surface of a three dimensional ball in four dimensions. He wanted this for philosophical reasons, so as to incorporate Mach's principle in a reasonable way. He stabilized his solution by introducing a cosmological constant, and when the universe was shown to be expanding, he retracted the constant as a blunder. This is not really much of a blunder — the cosmological constant is necessary within general relativity as it is currently understood, and it is widely believed to have a nonzero value today. Einstein took the wrong side in a few scientific debates.

- He briefly flirted with transverse and longitudinal mass concepts, before rejecting them.
- Einstein initially opposed Minkowski's geometrical formulation of special relativity, changing his mind completely a few years later.
- Based on his cosmological model, Einstein rejected expanding universe solutions by Friedman and Lemaitre as unphysical, changing his mind when the universe was shown to be expanding a few years later.
- Finding it too formal, Einstein believed that Heisenberg's matrix mechanics was incorrect. He changed his mind when Schrödinger and others demonstrated that the formulation in terms of the

Schrödinger equation, based on Einstein's wave-particle duality was equivalent to Heisenberg's matrices.

- Einstein rejected work on black holes by Chandrasekhar, Oppenheimer, and others, believing, along with Eddington, that collapse past the horizon (then called the 'Schwarzschild singularity') would never happen. So big was his influence, that this opinion was not rejected until the early 1960s, almost a decade after his death.

- Einstein believed that some sort of nonlinear instability could lead to a field theory whose solutions would collapse into pointlike objects which would behave like quantum particles. While there are many field theories with point-like particle solutions, none of them behave like quantum particles. It is widely believed that quantum mechanics would be impossible to reproduce from a local field theory of the type Einstein considered, because of Bell's inequality.

In addition to these well known mistakes, it is sometimes claimed that the general line of Einstein's reasoning in the 1905 relativity paper is flawed, or the photon paper, or one or another of the most famous papers. None of these claims are widely accepted.

Collaboration with Other Scientists

In addition to long time collaborators Leopold Infeld, Nathan Rosen, Peter Bergmann and others, Einstein also had some one-shot collaborations with various scientists.

Einstein-de Haas experiment

Einstein and De Haas demonstrated that magnetization is due to the motion of electrons, nowadays known to be the spin. In order to show this, they reversed the magnetization in an iron bar suspended on a torsion pendulum. They confirmed that this leads the bar to rotate, because the electron's angular momentum changes as the magnetization changes. This experiment needed to be sensitive, because the angular momentum associated with electrons is small, but it definitively established that electron motion of some kind is responsible for magnetization.

Schrödinger gas model

Einstein suggested to Erwin Schrödinger that he might be able to reproduce the statistics of a Bose-Einstein gas by considering a box. Then to each possible quantum motion of a particle in a box associate an independent harmonic oscillator. Quantizing these oscillators, each level will have an integer occupation number, which will be the number of particles in it.

This formulation is a form of second quantization, but it predates modern quantum mechanics. Erwin Schrödinger applied this to derive the thermodynamic properties of a semiclassical ideal gas. Schrödinger urged Einstein to add his name as co-author, although Einstein declined the invitation.

Einstein refrigerator

In 1926, Einstein and his former student Leó Szilárd co-invented (and in 1930, patented) the Einstein refrigerator. This Absorption refrigerator was then revolutionary for having no moving parts and using only heat as an input. On 11 November 1930, U.S. Patent 1,781,541 was awarded to Albert Einstein and Leó Szilárd for the refrigerator. Although the refrigerator was not immediately put into commercial production, the most promising of their patents being quickly bought up by the Swedish company Electrolux to protect its refrigeration technology from competition.

History

From 1926 until 1933 Einstein and Szilárd collaborated on ways to improve home refrigeration technology. The two were motivated by contemporary newspaper reports of a Berlin family who had been killed when a seal in their refrigerator broke and leaked toxic fumes into their home. Einstein and Szilárd proposed that a device without moving parts would eliminate the potential for seal failure, and explored practical applications for different refrigeration cycles. Einstein used the experience he had gained during his years at the Swiss Patent Office to apply for valid patents for their inventions in several countries, the two eventually being granted 45 patents in their names for three different models.

It has been suggested that most of the actual inventing was performed by Szilárd, with Einstein merely acting as a consultant and helping with the patent-related paperwork. Additionally, Einstein's name lent the research prestige and credibility.

The refrigerator was not immediately put into commercial production, the most promising of their patents being quickly bought up by the Swedish company Electrolux. A few demonstration units were constructed from other patents.

Operation

The machine is a single-pressure absorption refrigerator, similar in design to a gas absorption refrigerator. The refrigeration cycle uses ammonia pressure-equalizing fluid, butane refrigerant, and water absorbing fluid, has no moving parts, and does not require electricity to operate, needing only a heat source, e.g. a small gas burner or electric heating element.

The ammonia is introduced into the evaporator, causing the refrigerant to evaporate, taking energy from the surroundings, due to the fact that the partial pressure of the refrigerant is reduced, and the mix of gasses then passed through to a Condenser heat transfer condenser where it comes into contact with the absorption liquid. Since ammonia is soluble in water and butane is insoluble, the ammonia gas is absorbed by the water, freeing the butane. Heat is thus first given from the butane to the ammonia as the gasses mix, and then from the ammonia to the water, as the ammonia leaves the butane, taking heat with it, and dissolves into the water. The butane then assumes the pressure inside the condenser, which is enough to make it liquefy. Since butane's specific gravity is less than that of ammonia in solution in water, the liquid butane floats on top of the ammonia solution. The liquid butane then passes back to the evaporator to repeat the cycle. The ammonia solution flows to a heat exchanger where a heat source drives it from the water as a gas again and it returns to the evaporator.

The Einstein refrigerator has been described as "noiseless, inexpensive to produce and durable".

Present day

In September 2008 it was reported that Malcolm McCulloch of Oxford University was heading a three-year project to develop more robust appliances that could be used in locales lacking electricity, and that his team had completed a prototype Einstein refrigerator. He was quoted as saying that improving the design and changing the types of gases used might allow the design's efficiency to be quadrupled.

Bohr Vs Einstein

The Bohr-Einstein debates is a popular name given to a series of public disputes between Albert Einstein and Niels Bohr about quantum physics. These two men, along with Max Planck were the founders of the original quantum theory. Their "debates" are remembered because of their importance to the philosophy of science. Einstein sought a physics that would tell him what was happening in the real world "behind" the equations. Bohr was interested in the equations themselves and did not worry about an underlying reality.

Einstein's position with respect to quantum mechanics is significantly more subtle and open-minded than it has often been portrayed in technical manuals and popular science articles. His constant and powerful criticisms of quantum mechanics compelled its defenders to sharpen and refine their understanding of the philosophical and scientific implications of their own theory.

Pre-revolutionary Debates

Einstein was the first physicist to say that Planck's discovery of the quantum (h) would require a rewriting of physics. As though to prove his point, in 1905 he proposed that light sometimes acts as a particle which he called light quanta (now called the photon). Bohr was one of the most vocal opponents of the photon idea and did not openly embrace it until 1925. His later ability to work creatively with an idea he had so long resisted is quite unusual in the history of science. The photon appealed to Einstein because he saw it as a physical reality (although a confusing one) behind the numbers. Bohr disliked it because it made the choice of mathematical solution arbitrary. He did not like that a scientist had to choose between equations.

1913 brought the Bohr model of the hydrogen atom which made use of the quantum to explain the atomic spectrum. Einstein was at first dubious, but quickly changed his mind and embraced it. He tolerated Bohr's model despite the fact that its underlying reality could not be pictured in detail because he considered it a work in progress.

The Quantum revolution

The quantum revolution of the mid-1920s occurred under the direction of both Einstein and Bohr, and their post-revolutionary debates were about making sense of the change. The shocks for Einstein began in 1925 when Werner Heisenberg introduced matrix equations that removed the Newtonian elements of space and time from any underlying reality. The next shock came in 1926 when Max Born proposed that the mechanics was to be understood as a probability without any causal explanation. Finally, in late

1927, Heisenberg and Born declared at the Solvay Conference that the revolution was over and nothing further was needed. It was at that last stage that Einstein's skepticism turned to dismay. He believed that much had been accomplished, but the reasons for the mechanics still needed to be understood.

Einstein's refusal to accept the revolution as complete reflected his rejection of the idea that positions in space-time could never be completely known and by the way quantum probabilities did not reflect any underlying causes. He did not reject the statistics or probabilities on their own and Einstein himself was a great statistical thinker. It was the lack of any reason for an event that Einstein rejected. Bohr, meanwhile, was dismayed by none of the elements that troubled Einstein. He made his own peace with the contradictions by proposing a Principle of Complementarity that emphasized the role of the observer over the observed.

Post-Revolution: First stage

As mentioned above, Einstein's position underwent significant modifications over the course of the years. In the first stage, Einstein refuses to accept quantum indeterminism and seeks to demonstrate that the principle of indeterminacy can be violated, suggesting ingenious thought experiments which should permit the accurate determination of incompatible variables, such as position and velocity, or to explicitly reveal simultaneously the wave and the particle aspects of the same process.

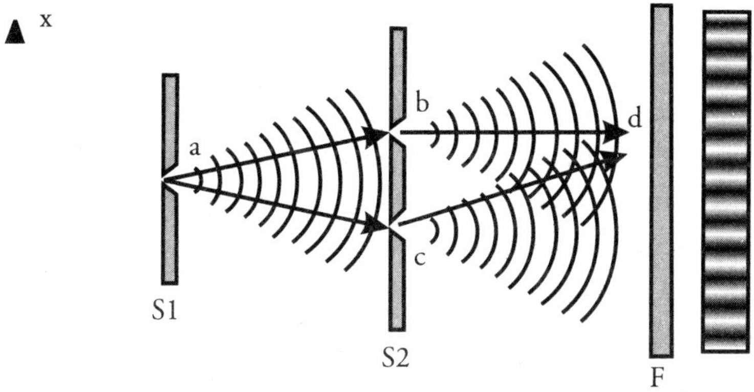

Figure A. A monochromatic beam (one for which all the particles have the same impulse) encounters a first screen, diffracts, and the diffracted wave encounters a second screen with two slits resulting in the formation of an interference figure on the background F. As always, it is assumed that only one particle at a time is able to pass the entire mechanism. From the measure of the recoil of the screen S1, according to Einstein, one can deduce from which slit the particle has passed without destroying the wave aspects of the process.

The first serious attack by Einstein on the "orthodox" conception took place during the *Fifth Conference of Physics* at the *Solvay Institute* in 1927. Einstein pointed out how it was possible to take advantage of the (universally accepted) laws of conservation of energy and of impulse (momentum) in order to obtain information on the state of a particle in a process of interference which, according to the principle of indeterminacy or that of complementarity, should not be accessible.

In order to follow his argumentation and to evaluate Bohr's response, it is convenient to refer to the experimental apparatus illustrated in figure A. A beam of light perpendicular to the *X* axis which propagates in the direction z encounters a screen S1 which presents a narrow (with respect to the wavelength of the ray) slit. After having passed through the slit, the wave function diffracts with an angular opening that causes it to encounter a second screen S2 which presents two slits. The successive propagation of the wave results in the formation of the interference figure on the final screen ***F***.

At the passage through the two slits of the second screen *S2*, the wave aspects of the process become essential. In fact, it is precisely the interference between the two terms of the quantum superposition corresponding to states in which the particle is localized in one of the two slits which implies that the particle is "guided" preferably into the zones of constructive interference and cannot end up in a point in the zones of destructive interference (in which the wave function is nullified). It is also important to note that any experiment designed to evidence the "corpuscular" aspects of the process at the passage of the screen *S2* (which, in this case, reduces to the determination of which slit the particle has passed through) inevitably destroys the wave aspects, implies the disappearance of the interference figure and the emergence of two concentrated spots of diffraction which confirm our knowledge of the trajectory followed by the particle.

At this point Einstein brings into play the first screen as well and argues as follows: since the incident particles have velocities (practically) perpendicular to the screen *S1*, and since it is only the interaction with this screen that can cause a deflection from the original direction of propagation, by the law of conservation of impulse which implies that the sum of the impulses of two systems which interact is conserved, if the incident particle is deviated toward the top, the screen will recoil toward the bottom and vice-versa. In realistic conditions the mass of the screen is so heavy that it will remain stationary, but, in principle, it is possible to measure even an infinitesimal recoil.

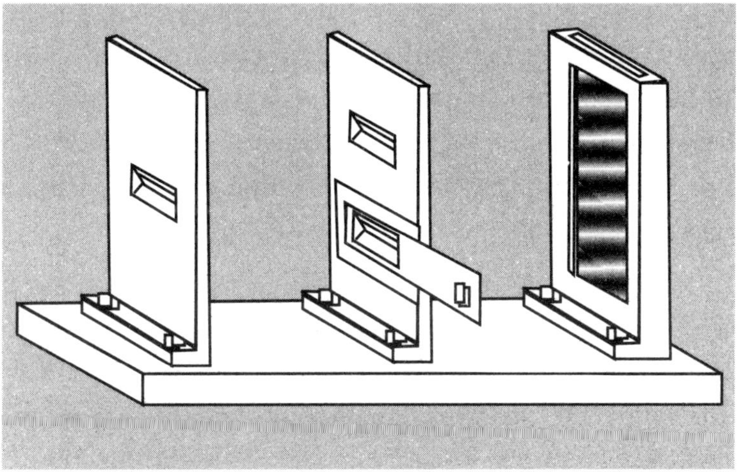

Figure B. Bohr's representation of Einstein's thought experiment described above. The mobile window is evidenced in order to underscore the fact that the attempt to know which slit a particle passes through destroys the interference pattern.

If we imagine taking the measurement of the impulse of the screen in the direction *X* after every single particle has passed, we can know, from the fact that the screen will be found recoiled toward the top (bottom), if the particle in question has been deviated toward the bottom (top) and therefore we can know from which slit in *S2* the particle has passed. But since the determination of the direction of the recoil of the screen after the particle has passed cannot influence the successive development of the process, we will still have an interference figure on the screen ***F***. The interference takes place precisely because the state of the system is the superposition of two states whose wave functions are non-Zero only near one of the two slits. On the other hand, if every particle passes through only the slit b or the slit c, then the set of systems is the statistical mixture of the two states, which means that interference is not possible. If Einstein is correct, then there is a violation of the principle of indeterminacy.

Bohr's response was to illustrate Einstein's idea more clearly via the diagrams in Figures B and C. Bohr observes that extremely precise knowledge of any (potential) vertical motion of the screen is an essential presupposition in Einstein's argument. In fact, if its velocity in the direction *X* before the passage of the particle is not known with a precision substantially greater than that induced by the recoil (that is, if it were already moving vertically with an unknown and greater velocity than that which it derives as a consequence of the contact with the particle), then the determination of its motion after the passage of the particle would not give the information we seek. However, Bohr continues, an extremely precise determination of the velocity of the screen, when one applies the principle of indeterminacy, implies an inevitable imprecision of its position in the direction X. Before the process even begins, the screen would therefore occupy an indeterminate position at least to a certain extent (defined by the formalism). Now consider, for example, the point d in figure A, where there is destructive interference. It's obvious that any displacement of the first screen would make the lengths of the two paths, *a-b-d* and *a-c-d*, different from those indicated in the figure. If the

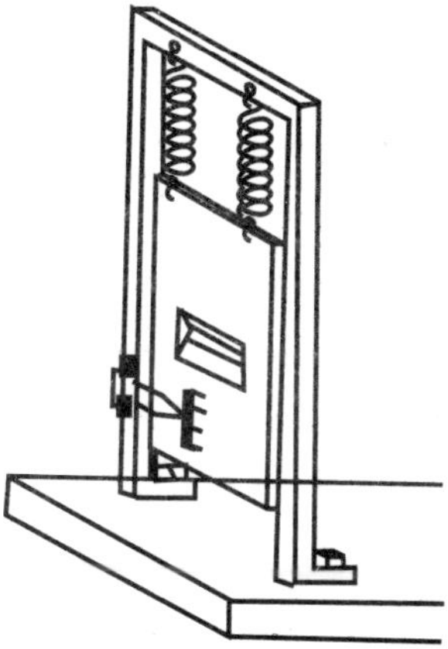

Figure C. In order to realize Einstein's proposal, it is necessary to replace the first screen in Figure 1 (S1) with a movable diaphragm which can move vertically such as this proposed by Bohr.

difference between the two paths varies by half a wavelength, at point d there will be constructive rather than destructive interference. The ideal experiment must average over all the possible positions of the screen *S1*, and, for every position, there corresponds, for a certain fixed point F, a different type of interference, from the perfectly destructive to the perfectly constructive. The effect of this averaging is that the pattern of interference on the screen F will be uniformly grey. Once more, our attempt to evidence the corpuscular aspects in S2 has destroyed the possibility of interference in F which depends crucially on the wave aspects.

It should be noted that, as Bohr recognized, for the understanding of this phenomenon "it is decisive that, contrary to genuine instruments of measurement, these bodies along with the particles would constitute, in the case under examination, the system to which the quantum-mechanical formalism must apply. With respect to the precision of the conditions under which one can correctly apply the formalism, it is essential to include the entire experimental apparatus. In fact, the introduction of any new apparatus, such as a mirror, in the path of a particle could introduce new effects of interference which influence essentially the predictions about the results which will be registered at the end."

Further along, Bohr attempts to resolve this ambiguity concerning which parts of the system should be considered macroscopic and which not:

In particular, it must be very clear that...the unambiguous use of spatiotemporal concepts in the description of atomic phenomena must be limited to the registration of observations which refer to images on a photographic lens or to analogous practically irreversible effects of amplification such as the formation of a drop of water around an ion in a dark room.

Bohr's argument about the impossibility of using the apparatus proposed by Einstein to violate the principle of indeterminacy depends crucially on the fact that a macroscopic system (the screen S1) obeys quantum laws. On the other hand, Bohr consistently asserted that, in order to illustrate the microscopic aspects of reality it is necessary to set off a process of amplification which involves macroscopic apparatuses, whose fundamental characteristic is that of obeying classical laws and which can be described in classical terms. This ambiguity would later come back in the form of what is still called today the measurement problem.

The principle of indeterminacy applied to time and energy

In many textbook examples and popular discussions of quantum mechanics, the principle of indeterminacy is explained by reference to the pair of variables position and velocity (or angular momentum). It is important to note that the wave nature of physical processes implies that there must exist another relation of indeterminacy: that between time and energy.

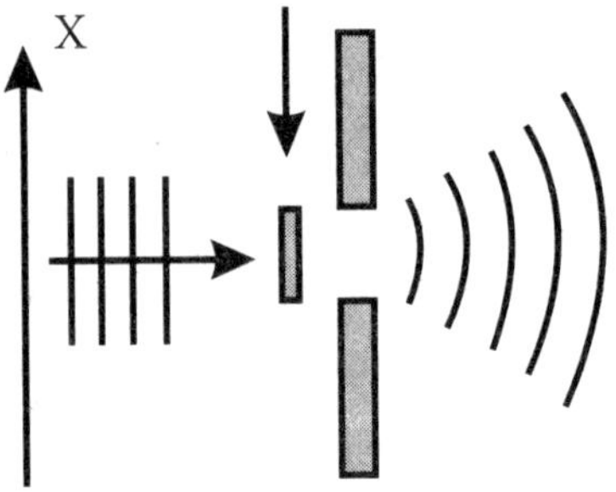

Figure D. A wave extended longitudinally passes through a slit which remains open only for a brief interval of time. Beyond the slit, there is a spatially limited wave in the direction of propagation.

In order to comprehend this relation, it is convenient to refer to the experiment illustrated in Figure D, which results in the propagation of a wave which is limited in spatial extension. Assume that, as illustrated in the figure, a ray which is extremely extended longitudinally is propagated toward a screen with a slit furnished with a shutter which remains open only for a very brief interval of time Dt. Beyond the slit, there will be a wave of limited spatial extension which continues to propagate toward the right.

A perfectly monochromatic wave (such as a note which cannot be divided into harmonics) is infinitely spatially extended. In order to have a wave which is limited in spatial extension (which is technically called a wave packet), several waves of different frequencies must be superimposed and distributed continuously within a certain interval of frequencies around an average value, such as ν_0;. It then happens that at a certain instant, there exists a spatial region (which translates with time) in which the contributions of the various fields of the superposition add up constructively. Nonetheless, according to a precise mathematical theorem, as we move far away from this region, the phases of the various fields, in any specified point, are distributed causally and destructive interference is produced. The region in which the wave is non-Zero is therefore spatially limited. It is easy to demonstrate that if the wave has a spatial extension equal to Δx (which means, in our example, that the shutter has remained open for a time $\Delta t = \Delta x / v$ where v is the velocity of the wave), then the wave contains (or is a superposition of) various monochromatic waves whose frequencies cover an interval $\Delta\nu$ which satisfies the relation:

$$\Delta\nu \geq \frac{1}{\Delta t}.$$

Remembering that in the universal relation of Planck, frequency and energy are proportional:

$$E = h\nu$$

...it follows immediately from the preceding inequality that the particle associated with the wave should possess an energy which is not perfectly defined (since different frequencies are involved in the superposition) and consequently there is indeterminacy in energy:

$$\Delta E = h\Delta\nu \geq \frac{h}{\Delta t}.$$

From this it follows immediately that:

$$\Delta E \Delta t \geq h$$

...which is the relation of indeterminacy between time and energy.

Einstein's second criticism

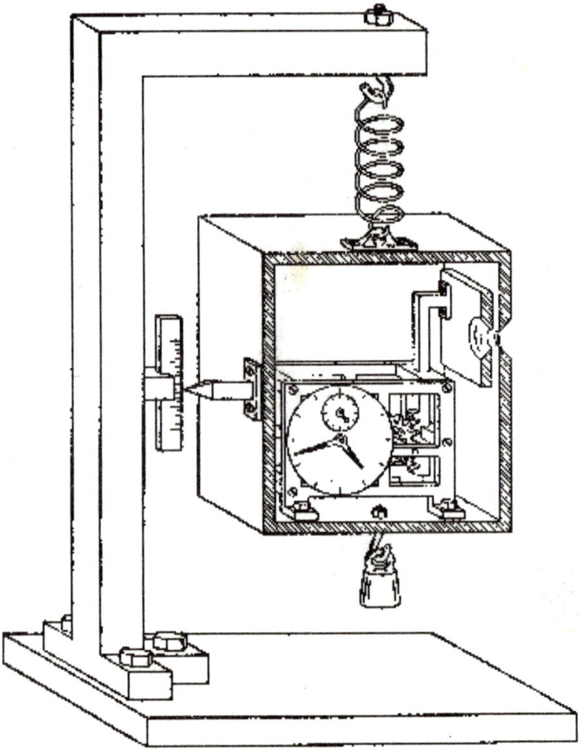

Einstein's thought experiment of 1930 as designed by Bohr. Einstein's box was supposed to prove the violation of the indeterminacy relation between time and energy.

At the sixth Congress of Solvay in 1930, the indeterminacy relation just discussed was Einstein's target of criticism. His idea contemplates the existence of an experimental apparatus which was subsequently designed by Bohr in such a way as to emphasize the essential elements and the key points which he would use in his response.

Einstein considers a box (called Einstein's box; see figure) containing electromagnetic radiation and a clock which controls the opening of a shutter which covers a hole made in one of the walls of the box. The shutter uncovers the hole for a time Δt which can be chosen arbitrarily. During the opening, we are to suppose that a photon, from among those inside the box, escapes through the hole. In this way, a wave of limited spatial extension has been created, following the explanation given above. In order to challenge the indeterminacy relation between time and energy, it is necessary to find a way to determine with an adequate precision, the energy that the photon has brought with it. At this point, Einstein turns to his celebrated relation between mass and energy of special relativity: $E = mc^2$. From this, it follows that knowledge of the mass of an object provides a precise indication about its energy. The argument is therefore very simple: if one weighs the box before and after the opening of the shutter and if a certain amount of energy has escaped from the box, the box will be lighter. The variation in mass multiplied by c_2 will provide precise knowledge of the energy emitted. Moreover, the clock will indicate the precise time at which the event of the particle's emission took place. Since, in principle, the mass of the box can be determined to an arbitrary degree of accuracy, the energy emitted can be determined with a precision ΔE as accurate as one desires. Therefore, the product $\Delta E \Delta t$ can be rendered less than what is implied by the principle of indeterminacy.

The idea is particularly acute and the argument seemed unassailable. It's important to consider the impact of all of these exchanges on the people involved at the time. Leon Rosenfeld, a scientist who had participated in the Congress, described the event several years later:

It was a real shock for Bohr...who, at first, could not think of a solution. For the entire evening he was extremely agitated, and he continued passing from one scientist to another, seeking to persuade them that it could not be the case, that it would have been the end of physics if Einstein were right; but he couldn't come up with any way to resolve the paradox. I will never forget the image of the two antagonists as they left the club: Einstein, with his tall and commanding figure, who walked tranquilly, with a mildly ironic smile, and Bohr who trotted along beside him, full of excitement... The morning after saw the triumph of Bohr.

The "triumph of Bohr" consisted in his demonstrating, once again, that Einstein's subtle argument was not conclusive, but even more so in the way that he arrived at this conclusion by appealing precisely to one of the great ideas of Einstein: the principle of equivalence between gravitational mass and inertial mass. Bohr showed that, in order for Einstein's experiment to function, the box would have to be suspended on a spring in the middle of a gravitational field. In order to obtain a measurement of weight, a pointer would have to be attached to the box which corresponded with the index on a scale. After the release of a photon, weights could be added to the box to restore it to its original position and this would allow us to determine the weight. But in order to return the box to its original position, the box itself would have to be measured. The inevitable uncertainty of the position of the box translates into an uncertainty in the position of the pointer and of the determination of weight and therefore of energy. On the other hand, since the system is immersed in a gravitational field which varies with the position, according to the principle of equivalence the uncertainty in the position of the clock implies an uncertainty with respect to its measurement of time and therefore of the value of the interval Δt. A precise evaluation of this effect leads to the conclusion that the relation $\Delta E \Delta t > h$, cannot be violated.

Post-Revolution: Second stage

The second phase of Einstein's "debate" with Bohr and the orthodox interpretation is characterized by an acceptance of the fact that it is, as a practical matter, impossible to simultaneously determine the values of certain incompatible quantities, but the rejection that this implies that these quantities do not actually have precise values. He rejects the probabilistic interpretation of Born and insists that quantum probabilities are epistemic and not ontological in nature. As a consequence, the theory must be incomplete in some way. He recognizes the great value of the theory, but suggests that it "does not tell the whole story," and, while providing an appropriate description at a certain level, it gives no information on the more fundamental underlying level:

I have the greatest consideration for the goals which are pursued by the physicists of the latest generation which go under the name of quantum mechanics, and I believe that this theory represents a profound level of truth, but I also believe that the restriction to laws of a statistical nature will turn out to be transitory.... Without doubt quantum mechanics has grasped an important fragment of the truth and will be a paragon for all future fundamental theories, for the fact that it must be deducible as a limiting case from such foundations, just as electrostatics is deducible from Maxwell's equations of the electromagnetic field or as thermodynamics is deducible from statistical mechanics.

These thoughts of Einstein's would set off a line of research into so-called hidden variable theories, such as the Bohm interpretation, in an attempt to complete the edifice of quantum theory. If quantum mechanics can be made complete in Einstein's sense, it cannot be done locally; this fact was demonstrated by John Stewart Bell with the formulation of Bell's inequality in 1964.

Post-Revolution: Third stage

Photon entanglement

Entanglement

Let us recall, for purposes of exposition, that a quantum system is described, at every instant, by a vector state which, according to the theory, represents the maximum amount of information that it is possible to have with respect to it. To simplify discussion, let's take the example of the state of polarization of a photon and associate with it the vector state $|45\rangle$. What does this information tell us about the properties of photons? The knowledge of the vector state, in fact, provides us exclusively with information on the possible results of measurements which we decide to carry out on the system. For example in the case just referred to, we know that if we were to apply a test for vertical polarization to the photon whose state is $|45\rangle$, it would have a probability of 1/2 of passing and 1/2 of failing. But the theory, which usually provides only probabilistic information on the results of hypothetical measurements, can, with reference to particular tests, assign the value *1* or *0* to the probability of obtaining specific results. So, in the case we are considering, the theory tells us that the photon has a probability of *1* of passing through a filter polarized at 45°, and a probability of *0* of passing through a filter polarized at *135*°. In this case, and with precise and exclusive reference to the observables (polarization at *45*° and *135*°) for which we know a *priori* the results of measurement, we can assert that the photon possesses the property in question: it is polarized at 45° or "possesses the property which guarantees that it will pass with certainty a test at *45°*." This is an important distinction with the situation in classical mechanics: in classical physics, any system always possesses precise values for all of the observables that we can conceive, but in quantum physics, a single system will indeed possess *some property*, but, with reference to other properties, we can do no better than make probabilistic prediction about the results of possible measurements, of and when they are actually executed. In a certain sense the theory teaches us that a system must not have too *many properties* and that, in particular, some are incompatible with others. So, for example, a photon that is "polarized at 45°" does not possess any definite property relative to vertical or horizontal polarization. This is important for understanding one of the fundamental assumptions on which the argument of Einstein, Podolsky and Rosen (or "EPR") is based:

(R)If, without disturbing a system in any way, it is possible to predict with certainty the result of the measurement of an observable of the system, then there exists an element of reality associated with the observable in question; the system "objectively possesses" the relative property.

Now consider the following situation: two photons are emitted by a source *S* and are propagated in two opposite directions. At a certain instant, one of them can be found in the region A, to the right of the source and the other in the region B symmetric to A with respect to S.

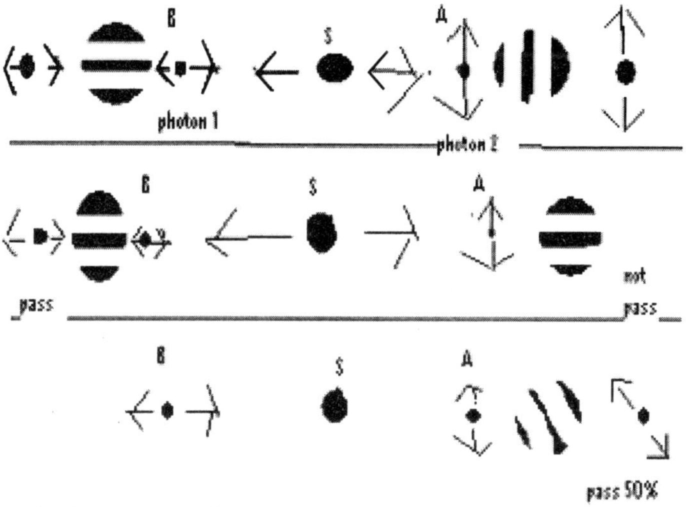

The behaviour, during various processes of measurement, of two distant photons as discussed in the text

We can call the photon at the right *1* and assume that it possesses a vertical polarization. This can be indicated as the vector state $|1,V\rangle$. Analogously, suppose that the photon on the left, indicated as *2*, has a horizontal polarization, so that it is described by the vector state $|2,H\rangle$. The entire system is described as the state

$$|\Psi\rangle = |1,V\rangle |2,H\rangle$$

...which corresponds to the single quantum state which asserts that "(one photon is in A with vertical polarization) and (one photon is in B with horizontal polarization)".

This state is called "factored" because it is, technically, the product of the two photons. Its properties are rather obvious and are illustrated in Figure G. For example if, given the state $|\Psi\rangle = |1,V\rangle|2,H\rangle$, we carry out a test of vertical polarization on the photon on the right and a test of horizontal polarization on the photon to the left, we know that both of them will pass with certainty. Similarly, if we carry out (center of figure) a test of horizontal polarization on both of the photons, the one on the right will certainly fail, while the one on the left will certainly pass. Lastly, consider the more general case in which the photon to the right is passed through a filter polarized at 45°. In this case, the photon 2 will pass through 1/2 of the time and end up polarized at *45°*, and it will fail to pass the other 1/2. The photon on the left has not been tested and therefore remains horizontally polarized.

The state $|1,V\rangle$ is actually a superposition of states, however, and must be rewritten as follows:

$$|1,V\rangle = \frac{1}{\sqrt{2}}|1,45\rangle + \frac{1}{\sqrt{2}}|1,135\rangle$$

Substituting this into the expression for the state $|\psi\rangle$, we have:

$$|\Psi\rangle = |1,V\rangle|2,H\rangle$$

$$= \frac{1}{\sqrt{2}}|1,45\rangle|2,H\rangle + \frac{1}{\sqrt{2}}|1,135\rangle|2,H\rangle$$

According to this formula, a measure of polarization at *45°* in A can result, with equal probability, in the photon *1* passing the test, in which case the system will be represented, according to wave packet reduction, as follows:

$$|\Psi\rangle = |1,V\rangle|2,H\rangle$$

$$= \frac{1}{\sqrt{2}}|1,45\rangle|2,H\rangle + \frac{1}{\sqrt{2}}|1,135\rangle|2,H\rangle$$

$$\Rightarrow |1,45\rangle|2,H\rangle$$

An important case is the one in which the photons have the same initial polarization:

$$|\Theta\rangle = |1,V\rangle|2,V\rangle$$

or

$$|\Lambda\rangle = |1,H\rangle|2,H\rangle$$

In order to understand entanglement, consider again the two photons discussed above and observe that that states and are both possible states of the system. But, if this is the case, then it follows that the superposition of the two states:

$$|\Psi\rangle = \frac{1}{\sqrt{2}}[|\Theta\rangle + |\Lambda\rangle]$$

$$= \frac{1}{\sqrt{2}}|1,V\rangle|2,V\rangle + \frac{1}{\sqrt{2}}|1,H\rangle|2,H\rangle$$

...is also a possible state of the system of two photons. What are the properties of this system?

It's immediately clear that each of the two photons does not possess the property of being polarized vertically or horizontally, since the probability of passing, for example, a test of vertical polarization on the part of photon *1* is characterized by the coefficient of the state in which it has this polarization and the square of this coefficient is one half. Therefore if one carries out this test, photon *1* will pass about half of the time in an unpredictable manner. The same reasoning applies to the horizontal test and for the other photon.

Suppose we are now interested in measuring the polarizations at *45°* and *135°*. We must express the state of vertical and horizontal polarizations as the superpositions of states of polarization at *45°* and *135°*. Substituting the appropriate expressions into the preceding formula and carrying out the explicit calculations, we have:

$$|\Psi\rangle = \frac{1}{\sqrt{2}}\frac{1}{\sqrt{2}}[|1,45\rangle + |1,135\rangle \frac{1}{\sqrt{2}}[|2,45\rangle + |2,135\rangle]$$

$$+\frac{1}{\sqrt{2}}[|1,45\rangle - |1,135\rangle]\frac{1}{\sqrt{2}}[|2,45\rangle - |2,135\rangle]$$

$$= \frac{1}{2}(\sqrt{2})[|1,45\rangle|2,45\rangle + |1,45\rangle|2,135\rangle + |1,135\rangle|2,45\rangle$$
$$+|1,135\rangle|2,135\rangle + |1,45\rangle|2,45\rangle - |1,45\rangle|2,135\rangle - |1,135\rangle$$
$$|2,45\rangle + |1,135\rangle|2,135\rangle$$

$$= \frac{1}{\sqrt{2}}|1,45\rangle|2,45\rangle + |1,135\rangle|2,135\rangle$$

The result is the superposition of the states of two photons polarized at 45° and of two polarized at 135°. The two new orthogonal directions have taken the place of the vertical and horizontal of the preceding expressions. This implies, of course, that every photon has a probability of 1/2 to pass a test of this type exactly as it has to pass the tests for vertical and horizontal polarization. If one were to continue and calculate the results for other possible measures of polarizations along arbitrary directions in the plane, it would eventually be noted that this result is generalizable as follows:

$$|\Psi\rangle = \frac{1}{\sqrt{2}}|1,n\rangle|2,n\rangle + \frac{1}{\sqrt{2}}|1,n\perp\rangle|2,n\perp\rangle$$

In words, this means that the state $|\psi\rangle$ always has the same form regardless of the directions chosen: it is the superposition of two states, in the first of which both of the photons are polarized in the chosen direction n, and in the second of which both of the photons are polarized on the orthogonal direction $n\perp$.

Now, suppose that an observer decides to carry out a measurement of the polarization of photon *1* along an arbitrarily chosen direction n. If the photon passes the test, then according to the principle of wave packet reduction, we have:

$$|\Psi\rangle = \frac{1}{\sqrt{2}}|1,n\rangle|2,n\rangle + \frac{1}{\sqrt{2}}|1,n\perp\rangle|2,n\perp\rangle$$

$$\Rightarrow |1,n\rangle|2,n\rangle$$

and the final state is factored. Spontaneously, photon *2*, which had no property of polarization before the measurement, has acquired a precise property as a result of the measurement of photon *1*! This is entanglement.

Applications

One important area where entanglement can be applied is in computer microchips. Normally, the size of a microchip is restricted by the wavelength of the photon carving the chip, being able to carve at one-half of the wavelength in accordance with the Rayleigh criterion. However, entangled photons can be separated and then rejoined together, and since they have exactly the same position the constructive interference doubles the energy so that it can carve as low as 1/4 of the original wavelength and thus make microelectronic devices half the size of what was previously possible. Entangling more than one photon can lead to even greater energies, hitting 1/6 and theoretically even 1/8 the original wavelength.

Instantaneous communication by means of quantum entanglement is actually impossible because neither side can manipulate the state of the entangled particles, they can only measure it. This fact means that if you measure one particle you cannot infer anything meaningful about the observers measuring the other particle, except you know what state they *will* measure, or have *already* measured. Thus, causality is preserved.

Photon entanglement may soon be used as a Covert channel if not already. This is due to it being impossible to eavesdrop on the channel, at least for now. Although it may be possible to entangle additional photons and thus observe the communication or tamper with it in the future, this would most likely require physical access to the photons. See the No cloning theorem for additional information.

It may soon be possible to mass produce entangled photons since scientists have discovered a way to produce these photons using a simple semi-conductor. This approach is not only simpler then the previous nonlinear optical crystals such as beta barium borate (BBO) or Potassium titanyl phosphate (KTP), but also produces them on demand as opposed to the one in ten billion being downconverted into entangled photons within the crystal. The semiconductor is made from gallium arsenide used in optoelectronics, and dots made from indium arsenide mere nanometers in size; this compound is convenient since it self organizes into dots. Currently it has to be produced at low temperatures to produce infrared light, but some companies predict that it can be produced at room temperature soon.

The argument of EPR

In 1935 Einstein, Boris Podolsky and Nathan Rosen developed an argument, published in the magazine Physical Review with the title *Can Quantum-Mechanical Description of Physical Reality Be Considered Complete?*, based on an entangled state of two systems. Before coming to this argument, it is necessary to formulate another hypothesis that comes out of Einstein's work in relativity: the idea of locality. *The elements of physical reality which are objectively possessed cannot be influenced instantaneously at a distance.*

The argument of EPR was in 1957 picked up by David Bohm and Yakir Aharonov in a paper published *in Physical Review* with the title *Discussion of Experimental Proof for the Paradox of Einstein, Rosen, and Podolsky.* The authors reformulated the argument in terms of an entangled state of two particles, which can be summarized as follows:

1) Consider a system of two photons which at time t are located, respectively, in the spatially distant regions A and B and which are also in the entangled state of polarization $|\Psi\rangle$ described above:

$$|\Psi,t\rangle = 1/\sqrt{2}\,|1,V\rangle|2,V\rangle + 1/\sqrt{2}\,|1,H\rangle|2,H\rangle$$

2) At time t the photon in region A is tested for vertical polarization. Suppose that the result of the measurement is that the photon passes through the filter. According to the reduction of the wave packet, the result is that, at time t+dt, the system becomes:

$$|\Psi,t+dt\rangle = |1,V\rangle|2,V\rangle$$

3) At this point, the observer in A who carried out the first measurement on photon *1*, without doing anything else that could disturb the system or the other photon, can predict with certainty that photon *2* will pass a test of vertical polarization. From assumption (R), it follows that photon 2

possesses an element of physical reality: that of having a vertical polarization.

4) According to the assumption of locality, it cannot have been the action carried out in A which created this element of reality for photon *2*. Therefore, we must conclude that the photon possessed the property of being able to pass the vertical polarization test *before* and *independently* of the measurement of photon *1*.

5) At time t, the observer in *A* could have decided to carry out a test of polarization at *45°*, obtaining a certain result, for example, that the photon passes the test. In that case, he could have concluded that photon *2* turned out to be polarized at *45°*. Alternatively, if the photon did not pass the test, he could have concluded that photon *2* turned out to be polarized at *135°*. Combining one of these alternatives with the conclusion reached in *4*, it seems that photon *2*, before the measurement took place, possessed both the property of being able to pass with certainty a test of vertical polarization and the property of being able to pass with certainty a test of polarization at either *45°* or *135°*. These properties are incompatible according to the formalism.

6) Since natural and obvious requirements have forced the conclusion that photon *2* simultaneously possesses incompatible properties, this means that, even if it is not possible to determine these properties simultaneously and with arbitrary precision, they are nevertheless possessed

objectively by the system. But quantum mechanics denies this possibility and it is therefore an incomplete theory.

Bohr's response

Bohr's response to this fascinating and elegant argument was published, five months later than the original publication of EPR, in the same magazine *Physical Review* and with the exact same title as the original. The crucial point of Bohr's answer is distilled in a passage which he later had republished in Paul Arthur Schilpp's book *Albert Einstein, scientist-philosopher* in honor of the seventieth birthday of Einstein. Bohr attacks assumption (R) of EPR by stating:

the statement of the criterion in question is ambiguous with regard to the expression "without disturbing the system in any way". Naturally, in this case no mechanical disturbance of the system under examination can take place in the crucial stage of the process of measurement. But even in this stage there arises the essential problem of an influence on the precise conditions which define the possible types of prediction which regard the subsequent behaviour of the system...their arguments do not justify their conclusion that the quantum description turns out to be essentially incomplete... This description can be characterized as a rational use of the possibilities of an unambiguous interpretation of the process of measurement compatible with the finite and uncontrollable interaction between the object and the instrument of measurement in the context of quantum theory.

As John Bell later pointed out, this passage is almost unintelligible. What does Bohr mean, Bell asks, by the specification "mechanical" that is used to refer to the "disturbances" that Bohr maintains should not be taken into consideration? What is meant by the expression "an influence on the precise conditions" if not that different measurements in A provide different information on the system in B? This fact is not only admitted but is an essential part of the argument of EPR. Lastly, what could Bohr have meant by the expression "uncontrollable interaction between the object and the measuring apparatus", considering that the central point of the argument of EPR is the hypothesis that, if one accepts locality, only the part of the system in A can be disturbed by the process of measurement and that, notwithstanding this fact, this process provides precise information on the part of the system in B? Is Bohr already contemplating the possibility of "spooky action at a distance?" If so, why not declare it explicitly? If one abandons the assumption of locality, the argument of EPR obviously collapses immediately.

In any case, very few among the illustrious protagonists of the debate on the foundations of quantum theory were able to grasp the true sense of the profound analysis of Einstein. Pauli dismissed it with a few words and Born completely misinterpreted it. But Einstein's defeat represents one of the highest points of scientific research in the first half of the twentieth century because it called attention to an element of quantum theory, quantum non-locality, which is absolutely central to our modern understanding of the physical world.

Post-Revolution: Fourth stage

In his last writing on the topic, Einstein further refined his position, making it completely clear that what really disturbed him about the quantum theory was the problem of the total renunciation of all minimal standards of realism, even at the microscopic level, that the acceptance of the completeness of the theory implied. Although the majority of experts in the field seem to accept the Copenhagen interpretation, there are critics who, like Einstein, believe that it has failed to provide a sensible and acceptable representation of reality.

Religious Views of Albert Einstein

The religious views of Albert Einstein have been studied in detail by scholars of religion in order to obtain relevant perspectives on the relationship between religion and science.

Theological determinism

The question of scientific determinism gave rise to questions about Einstein's position on theological determinism, and whether or not he believed in God, or in a god. In 1929, Einstein told Rabbi Herbert S. Goldstein "I believe in Spinoza's God, who reveals Himself in the lawful harmony of the world, not in a God Who concerns Himself with the fate and the doings of mankind."

Agnosticism

In a 1950 letter to M. Berkowitz, Einstein stated that "My position concerning God is that of an agnostic. I am convinced that a vivid consciousness of the primary importance of moral principles for the betterment and ennoblement of life does not need the idea of a law-giver, especially a law-giver who works on the basis of reward and punishment." One might compare this to Deism or the religious stance of Carl Jung.

Disbelief in a personal god

Einstein also stated: "I have repeatedly said that in my opinion the idea of a personal God is a childlike one. You may call me an agnostic, but I do not share the crusading spirit of the professional atheist whose fervor is mostly due to a painful act of liberation from the fetters of religious indoctrination received in youth." He also said in a conversation with Hubertus, Prince of Löwenstein-Wertheim-Freudenberg, "In view of such harmony in the cosmos which I, with my limited human mind, am able to recognize, there are yet people who say there is no God. But what really makes me angry is that they quote me for the support of such views."

Admiration for structure

Einstein clarified his religious views in a letter he wrote in response to those who claimed that he worshipped a conventional god: "It was, of course, a lie what you read about my religious convictions, a lie which is being systematically repeated. I do not believe in a personal god and I have never denied this but have expressed it clearly. If something is in me which can be called religious then it is the unbounded admiration for the structure of the world so far as our science can reveal it." In his book The World as *I See* It, he wrote:

"A knowledge of the existence of something we cannot penetrate, of the manifestations of the profoundest reason and the most radiant beauty, which are only accessible to our reason in their most elementary forms-it is this knowledge and this emotion that constitute the truly religious attitude; in this sense, and in this alone, I am a deeply religious man."

Three styles of religious belief

In a 1930 *New York* Times article, Einstein distinguished three styles which are usually intermixed in actual religious belief. A poor understanding of causality causes fear, and the fearful invent supernatural beings. The desire for love and support create a social and moral need for a supreme being; both these styles have an anthropomorphic concept of God. The third style, which Einstein deemed most mature, originates in a deep sense of awe and mystery. He said, "The individual feels . . . the sublimity and marvelous order which reveal themselves in nature . . . and he wants to experience the universe as a single significant whole." Einstein saw science as an antagonist of the first two styles of religious belief, but as a partner of the third style. As he wrote later, "[E]ven though the realms of religion and science in themselves are clearly marked off from each other" there are "strong reciprocal relationships and dependencies . . . science without religion is lame, religion without science is blind . . . a legitimate conflict between science and religion cannot exist."

Humanism

Einstein was also a Humanist and a supporter of Ethical Culture. He served on the advisory board of the First Humanist Society of New York. For the seventy-fifth anniversary of the *New York Society for Ethical Culture,* he noted that the idea of Ethical Culture embodied his personal conception of what is most valuable and enduring in religious idealism. He observed, "Without 'ethical culture' there is no salvation for humanity." He was an honorary associate of the British Humanist organisation, the Rationalist Press Association and its journal was among the items present on his desk at his death.

Enlightenment and liberation

Einstein published a paper in *Nature* in 1940 entitled "Science and Religion" in which he wrote:

...a person who is religiously enlightened appears to me to be one who has, to the best of his ability, liberated himself from the fetters of his selfish desires and is preoccupied with thoughts, feelings and aspirations to which he clings because of their super-personal value ... regardless of whether any attempt is made to unite this content with a Divine Being, for otherwise it would not be possible to count Buddha and Spinoza as religious personalities. Accordingly a religious person is devout in the sense that he has no doubt of the significance of those super-personal objects and goals which neither require nor are capable of

rational foundation ... In this sense religion is the age-old endeavour of mankind to become clearly and completely conscious of these values and goals, and constantly to strengthen their effects." He argued that conflicts between science and religion "have all sprung from fatal errors".

An understanding of causality was fundamental to religious belief. In Einstein's view, "neither the rule of human nor Divine Will exists as an independent cause of natural events. To be sure, the doctrine of a personal God interfering with natural events could never be *refuted* . . . by science, for [it] can always take refuge in those domains in which scientific knowledge has not yet been able to set foot.

Einstein and the Catholic Church

Einstein has been cited by defenders of Pope Pius XII for a statement he allegedly made in a 1940 article for TIME magazine. He was quoted by the newsweekly as saying that the Church was the only notable institution that stood against the rise of the Third Reich and its campaign to suppress truth. However, skeptics have argued that the statement is poorly sourced and that it doesn't necessarily reflect Einstein's views on the matter.

In a 1954 letter to American secularist writer Paul Blanshard, he criticized the Catholic Church's opposition to birth control, saying it would be detrimental to the general population, at a time when there were growing fears about the overpopulation of the planet Earth.

Human weakness

In a 1954 letter to Eric Gutkind, Einstein wrote:

. . . The word God is for me nothing more than the expression and product of human weaknesses, the Bible a collection of honourable, but still primitive legends which are nevertheless pretty childish. No interpretation no matter how subtle can (for me) change this. These . . . interpretations are highly manifold according to their nature and have almost nothing to do with the original text. For me the Jewish religion like all other religions is an incarnation of the most childish superstitions. And the Jewish people to whom I gladly belong and with whose mentality I have a deep affinity have no different quality for me than all other people. As far as my experience goes, they are also no better than other human groups, although they are protected from the worst cancers by a lack of power. Otherwise I cannot see anything 'chosen' about them.

Einstein had previously explored this belief that man could not understand the nature of God when he gave an interview to Time Magazine explaining:-

I'm not an atheist. I don't think I can call myself a pantheist. The problem involved is too vast for our limited minds. We are in the position of a little child entering a huge library filled with books in many languages. The child knows someone must have written those books. It does not know how. It does not understand the languages in which they are written. The child dimly suspects a mysterious order in the arrangement of the books but doesn't know what it is. That, it seems to me, is the attitude of even the most intelligent human being toward God. We see the universe marvelously arranged and obeying certain laws but only dimly understand these laws.

Political Views of Albert Einstein

The political views of Albert Einstein emerged publicly in the middle of the 20th century due to latter's fame and reputation for genius, who offered and was called on to give judgments and opinions on matters often unrelated to theoretical physics or mathematics.

Humanitarian involvement

With increasing public demands, his involvement in political, humanitarian, and academic projects in various countries, and his new acquaintances with scholars and political figures from around the world, Einstein was less able to achieve the productive isolation that he needed in order to work.

Einstein was not timid, and he was aware of the world around him, with no illusion that ignoring politics would make world events fade away. His very visible position allowed him to speak and write frankly, even provocatively, at a time when many people of conscience could only flee to the underground or keep doubts about developments within their own movements to themselves for fear of internecine fighting.

Einstein flouted the ascendant Nazi movement, tried to be a voice of moderation in the tumultuous formation of the State of Israel and braved anti-communist politics and resistance to the civil rights movement in the United States. He participated in the 1927 congress of the League against Imperialism in Brussels.

Zionism

Einstein was a socialist Zionist who supported the creation of a Jewish national homeland in the British mandate of Palestine. In 1931, The Macmillan Company published About Zionism: Speeches and Lectures by Professor Albert Einstein. Querido, an Amsterdam publishing house, collected eleven of Einstein's essays into a 1933 book entitled Mein Weltbild, translated to English as The World as I See It; Einstein's foreword dedicates the collection "to the Jews of Germany". In the face of Germany's rising militarism, Einstein wrote and spoke for peace.

Einstein publicly stated reservations about the proposal to partition the British-supervised British Mandate of Palestine into independent Arab and Jewish countries. In a 1938 speech, "Our Debt to Zionism", he said: "My awareness of the essential nature of Judaism resists the idea of a Jewish state with borders, an army, and a measure of temporal power, no matter how modest. I am afraid of the inner damage Judaism will sustain-especially from the development of a narrow nationalism within our own ranks, against which we have already had to fight strongly, even without a Jewish state. ... If external necessity should after all compel us to assume this burden, let us bear it with tact and patience." In a 1947 letter to Indian Prime Minister Jawaharlal Nehru, Einstein stated that the Balfour Declaration's proposal to establish a national home for Jews in Palestine "redresses the balance" of justice and history.

The United Nations did divide the mandate, demarcating the borders of several new countries including the State of Israel, and war broke out immediately. Einstein was one of the authors of an open letter to the New York Times in 1948 criticizing Menachem Begin's Herut (Freedom) Party for the Deir Yassin massacre (Einstein et al. 1948).

Einstein served on the Board of Governors of The Hebrew University of Jerusalem. In his Will of 1950, Einstein bequeathed literary rights to his writings to The Hebrew University, where many of his original documents are held in the Albert Einstein Archives.

When President Chaim Weizmann died in 1952, Einstein was asked to be Israel's second president, but he declined, stating that he had "neither the natural ability nor the experience to deal with human beings." He wrote: "I am deeply moved by the offer from our State of Israel, and at once saddened and ashamed that I cannot accept it."

Anti-Nazism

Einstein had moved to the United States in December 1932, where he had been at the California Institute of Technology in Pasadena, California, and also was a guest lecturer at Abraham Flexner's newly founded Institute for Advanced Study in Princeton, New Jersey.

During the 1930s and into World War II, Einstein wrote affidavits recommending United States visas for European Jews who were trying to flee persecution. He raised money for Zionist organizations and was, in part, responsible for the 1933 formation of the International Rescue Committee.

In Germany, Deutsche Physik activists published pamphlets and even textbooks denigrating Einstein. Nobel laureates Philipp Lenard and Johannes Stark led a campaign to eliminate Einstein's work from the German lexicon as unacceptable "Jewish physics" (Jüdische Physik). Instructors who taught his theories were blacklisted, including Nobel laureate Werner Heisenberg, who had debated quantum probability with Bohr and Einstein. Philipp Lenard claimed that the mass-energy equivalence formula needed to be credited to Friedrich Hasenöhrl to make it an Aryan creation. A man convicted of conspiring to kill Einstein was fined a mere six dollars.

Atomic bomb

Concerned scientists, many of them refugees from European anti-Semitism in the U.S., recognized the danger of German scientists developing an atomic bomb based on the newly discovered phenomena of nuclear fission. In 1939, the Hungarian émigré Leó Szilárd, having failed to arouse U.S. government interest on his own, worked with Einstein to write a letter to U.S. President Franklin Delano Roosevelt, which Einstein signed, urging U.S. development of such a weapon. On 11 October 1939 Alexander Sachs, an adviser to Roosevelt on economic affairs, delivered the Einstein-Szilárd letter and persuaded the president of its importance. "This requires action", Roosevelt told an aide, and authorized secret research into the harnessing of nuclear fission for military purposes.

By 1942 this effort had become the Manhattan Project, the largest secret scientific endeavor undertaken up to that time. By late 1945, the U.S. had developed operational nuclear weapons, and used them on the Japanese cities of Hiroshima and Nagasaki. Einstein himself did not play a role in the development of the atomic bomb other than signing the letter although he did help the United States Navy with some unrelated theoretical questions it was working on during the war.

According to Linus Pauling, Einstein later expressed regret about his letter to Roosevelt. In 1947, Einstein wrote an article for The Atlantic Monthly arguing that the United States should not try to pursue an atomic monopoly, and instead should equip the United Nations with nuclear weapons for the sole purpose of maintaining deterrence.

Cold War Era

When he was a visible figure working against the rise of Nazism, Einstein had sought help and developed working relationships in both the West and what was to become the Soviet bloc. After World War II, enmity between the former allies became a very serious issue for people with international résumés. To make things worse, during the first days of McCarthyism Einstein was writing about a single world government; it was at this time that he wrote, "I do not know how the third World War will be fought, but I can tell you what they will use in the Fourth — rocks!" In a 1949 Monthly Review article entitled "Why Socialism?" Albert Einstein described a chaotic capitalist society, a source of evil to be overcome, as the "predatory phase of human development" (Einstein 1949). With Albert Schweitzer and Bertrand Russell, Einstein lobbied to stop nuclear testing and future bombs. Days before his death, Einstein signed the Russell-Einstein Manifesto, which led to the Pugwash Conferences on Science and World Affairs.

Einstein was a member of several civil rights groups, including the Princeton chapter of the NAACP. When the aged W. E. B. Du Bois was accused of being a Communist spy, Einstein volunteered as a character witness, and the case was dismissed shortly afterward. Einstein's friendship with activist Paul Robeson, with whom he served as co-chair of the American Crusade to End Lynching, lasted twenty years.

In 1946, Einstein collaborated with Rabbi Israel Goldstein, Middlesex University heir C. Ruggles Smith, and activist attorney George Alpert on the Albert Einstein Foundation for Higher Learning, which was formed to create a Jewish-sponsored secular university, open to all students, on the grounds of the former Middlesex University in Waltham, Massachusetts.

Middlesex was chosen in part because it was accessible from both Boston and New York City, Jewish cultural centers of the U.S. Their vision was a university "deeply conscious both of the Hebraic tradition of Torah looking upon culture as a birthright, and of the American ideal of an educated democracy." The collaboration was stormy, however. Finally, when Einstein wanted to appoint British economist Harold Laski as the university's president, George Alpert wrote that Laski was "a man utterly alien to American principles of democracy, tarred with the Communist brush." Einstein withdrew his support and barred the use of his name. The university opened in 1948 as Brandeis University. In 1953, Brandeis offered Einstein an honorary degree, but he declined.

Given Einstein's links to Germany and Zionism, his socialist ideals, and his links to Communist figures, the U.S. Federal Bureau of Investigation kept a file on Einstein that grew to 1,427 pages. Many of the documents in the file were sent to the FBI by concerned citizens: Some objected to his immigration, while others asked the FBI to protect him.

Death

On 17 April 1955, Albert Einstein experienced internal bleeding caused by the rupture of an abdominal aortic aneurysm, which had previously been reinforced surgically by Dr. Rudolph Nissen in 1948. He took the draft of a speech he was preparing for a television appearance commemorating the State of Israel's seventh anniversary with him to the hospital, but he did not live long enough to complete it. Einstein refused surgery, saying: "I want to go when I want. It is tasteless to prolong life artificially. I have done my share, it is time to go. I will do it elegantly." He died in Princeton Hospital early the next morning at the age of 76, having continued to work until near the end. Einstein's remains were cremated and his ashes were scattered around the grounds of the Institute for Advanced Study, Princeton, New Jersey. During the autopsy, the pathologist of Princeton Hospital, Thomas Stoltz Harvey removed Einstein's brain for preservation, without the permission of his family, in hope that the neuroscience of the future would be able to discover what made Einstein so intelligent.

Legacy

While travelling, Einstein had written daily to his wife Elsa and adopted stepdaughters, Margot and Ilse, and the letters were included in the papers bequeathed to The Hebrew University. Margot Einstein permitted the personal letters to be made available to the public, but requested that it not be done until twenty years after her death (she died in 1986). Barbara Wolff, of The Hebrew University's Albert Einstein Archives, told the BBC that there are about 3,500 pages of private correspondence written between 1912 and 1955.

The United States' National Academy of Sciences commissioned the Albert Einstein Memorial, a monumental bronze and marble sculpture by Robert Berks, dedicated in 1979 at its Washington, D.C. campus adjacent to the National Mall.

Einstein bequeathed the royalties from use of his image to The Hebrew University of Jerusalem. Corbis, successor to The Roger Richman Agency, licenses the use of his name and associated imagery, as agent for the Hebrew University.

Albert Einstein in Popular Culture

Albert Einstein has been the subject of or inspiration for many works of popular culture.

On Einstein's 72nd birthday in 1951, UPI photographer Arthur Sasse was trying to persuade him to smile for the camera, but having smiled for photographers many times that day, Einstein stuck out his tongue instead. This photo became one of the most popular photos ever taken of Einstein and it is well recognized in popular culture, often used in merchandise depicting Einstein in a lighthearted sense. On June 19, 2009, the photograph was sold at auction for $74,324, a record for an Einstein picture.

"Einstein" has become a word used to describe someone extremely intelligent; the name is also applied sarcastically to someone who states the obvious or displays a lack of intelligence or insight ("Way to go, Einstein!").

Albert Einstein has been the subject of or inspiration for many novels, films and plays, such as Yahoo Serious's intentionally inaccurate biography of Einstein as a Tasmanian in the film Young Einstein, Jean-Claude Carrier's 2005 French novel, Einstein S'il Vous Plaît ("Einstein If You Please), Alan Lightman's collection of short stories Einstein's Dreams, and Steve Martin's comedic play Picasso at the Lapin Agile. He was the subject of Philip Glass's groundbreaking 1976 opera Einstein on the Beach and his humorous side is the subject of Ed Metzger's one-man play Albert Einstein: The Practical Bohemian. He was also the subject of the 1994 romantic comedy I.Q. where he was portrayed by Walter Matthau. In the film A.I.: Artificial Intelligence he was portrayed as a holographic personality called Dr. Know (voiced by Robin Williams). He was also portrayed in the real-time strategy game Command & Conquer: Red Alert. Most recently, he was the subject (along with Arthur Eddington) of the BBC Two film Einstein and Eddington, featuring David Tennant as Eddington and Andy Serkis as Einstein, and detailing Einstein's development of his theories and Eddington's attempts to prove them. A holographic representation of Einstein, played by Jim Norton appeared in two episodes of Star Trek: The Next Generation.

Einstein is a favorite model for depictions of mad scientists and absent-minded professors; his expressive face and distinctive hairstyle have been widely copied and exaggerated. The Star Wars character Yoda's eyes were modeled after Einstein's. Time magazine's Frederic Golden wrote that Einstein was "a cartoonist's dream come true."

Albert Einstein is one of the celebrities immortalized on the cover of the Beatles' Sgt. Pepper's Lonely Hearts Club Band. A verse of James Taylor's song Secret O' Life mentions Einstein and his special theory of relativity. Kerry Livgren of the progressive rock band Kansas stated that he wrote the song "Portrait (He Knew)" about Einstein. Mariah Carey's most recent album is titled $E=MC^2$ after Einstein's celebrated equation.

The scientist is widely mentioned on lists of left-handed people but several photographs show him using his right hand to hold pens or chalk.

In the movie Back to the Future, the character of Dr. Emmett Brown, portrayed as a brilliant scientist, time traveler and inventor, has a dog called "Einstein", named after his Doc Brown's favorite scientist.

Awards and Honours

In 1922, Einstein was awarded the 1921 Nobel Prize in Physics, "for his services to Theoretical Physics, and especially for his discovery of the law of the photoelectric effect". This refers to his 1905 paper on the photoelectric effect, "On a Heuristic Viewpoint Concerning the Production and Transformation of Light", which was well supported by the experimental evidence by that time. The presentation speech began by mentioning "his theory of relativity [which had] been the subject of lively debate in philosophical circles [and] also has astrophysical implications which are being rigorously examined at the present time." (Einstein 1923)

It was long reported that Einstein gave the Nobel prize money directly to his first wife, Mileva Maric, in compliance with their 1919 divorce settlement. However, personal correspondence made public in 2006 shows that he invested much of it in the United States, and saw much of it wiped out in the Great Depression.

Einstein traveled to New York City in the United States for the first time on 2 April, 1921. When asked where he got his scientific ideas, Einstein explained that he believed scientific work best proceeds from an examination of physical reality and a search for underlying axioms, with consistent explanations that apply in all instances and avoid contradicting each other. He also recommended theories with visualizable results (Einstein 1954).

In 1999, Albert Einstein was named Person of the Century by Time magazine, a Gallup poll recorded him as the fourth most admired person of the 20th century in the U.S. and according to The 100: A Ranking of the Most Influential Persons in History, Einstein is "the greatest scientist of the twentieth century and one of the supreme intellects of all time."

Albert Einstein has been recognized many times over for his achievements. The International Union of Pure and Applied Physics named 2005 the "World Year of Physics" in commemoration of the 100th anniversary of the publication of the Annus Mirabilis Papers.

The Albert Einstein Memorial in central Washington, D.C. is a monumental bronze statue depicting Einstein seated with manuscript papers in hand. The statue is located in a grove of trees at the southwest corner of the grounds of the National Academy of Sciences on Constitution Avenue, near the Vietnam Veterans Memorial.

The chemical element 99, einsteinium, was named for him in August 1955, four months after Einstein's death.

In 1999, Time magazine named him the Person of the Century, beating contenders like Mahatma Gandhi and Franklin Roosevelt, and in the words of a biographer, "to the scientifically literate and the public at large, Einstein is synonymous with genius."

2001 Einstein is an inner main belt asteroid discovered on 5 March 1973.

The Albert Einstein Award (sometimes called the Albert Einstein Medal because it is accompanied with a gold medal) is an award in theoretical physics, that was established to recognize high achievement in the natural sciences.

The Albert Einstein Peace Prize is an award that is given yearly by the Chicago, Illinois-based Albert Einstein Peace Prize Foundation. Winners of the prize receive $50,000.

In 1990, his name was added to the Walhalla temple, east of Regensburg, in Bavaria, Germany.